Computer Architecture & Programming of the Intel x86 Family

Patrick H. Stakem

(C) 1988, 2013

Expanded, Updated, and Revised

3rd Edition, 5th in series, Computer Architecture

ISBN-9781520263724

Table of Contents

Introduction

This book is an introduction to computer architecture, hardware and software, presented in the context of the Intel x86 family. The x86 describes not only a line of microprocessor chips dating back to 1978, but also an instruction set architecture (ISA) that the chips implement. The chip families were built by Intel and other manufacturers, and execute the same instructions, but in different manners. The results are the same, arithmetically and logically, but may differ in their timing.

Why the focus on the Intel x86? It was the basis of the IBM personal computer (PC) family and its spin-offs. It has transitioned from a 16 to a 32 to a 64-bit architecture, keeping compatibility for more than 30 years. It's an de-facto industry standard that has withstood the test of time.

The purpose of this book is to provide the basic background information for an understanding of the 80x86 family, the IBM Personal Computer (pc), and programming in assembly language as an introduction to the broader field of Computer Architecture. It will stress the pervasiveness of this pc-based technology in everyday things and events. It will provide an introduction to Software System Engineering and the Design for Debugging methodology. This book is a spin-off of a course in Computer Architecture/System Integration, taught in the graduate Engineering Science Program at Loyola College (now, Loyola University in Maryland).

The personal computer revolution has touched all aspects of daily life. Microelectronics and pc's have provided us with a new set of tools. Pc's, both as manufactured goods and as manufacturing tools, took on an increasingly large role in the world economy. We have become an information (handling) society.

Every currently manufactured automobile, airplane, or consumer good, from washers and dryers to radial arm saws, are microprocessor based. Every service, banking, fast food, supermarkets, legal services, medical, etc. use computers based on microprocessors. Some of these computers are visible and obvious, and some are embedded in the system, hard to see.

Pc's and microelectronics provide an enabling technology; we can do more than we could before. Unfortunately, we have developed into two classes:

pc literate and pc non-literate. One must master this technology or be mastered by it.

A pc then is a computer I have on my desk, and a mainframe is a computer I can't lift. A server spends most of its time providing services (data, internet) to other computers.

How do we get a computer to do what we want? A big stick is sometimes a help. The early computers in the late 1940's and early 1950's were wired by plugboards for the sequence of instructions, and the numeric data was set in by switches. The program was run, results were obtained, and changes made to the configuration for new tasks. Faulty vacuum tubes were identified and replaced. This was a rather time consuming process.

The issue was in finding a common language for people to tell computers what specifically to do. Computers are good at math and logic, so the language would reflect that. Humans are good at ambiguity, and that needs to be eliminated. Procedural languages and formula languages (Fortran) became popular. The higher level languages such as c, Pascal, Java, LISP, and Cobol evolved to let people describe algorithms and processes to machinery that would then implement these. The languages were human-oriented, and process-oriented. The computers didn't understand them, and the people struggled with them.

Computers better understand an assembly language, which has a one to one correspondence with their basic instruction set. This inherent instruction set is architected to take advantage of the computer hardware. It is difficult, but not impossible, for people to write a program in this assembly language. Worse, the language is different for each processor type. However, the assembly language matches the underlying hardware architecture and organization. The human programmers are forced into speaking the computer's language.

From the standpoint of Computer Science, we can program in a higher order language and implement algorithms, without worrying how they get implemented. From a Computer Engineering standpoint, we want to have some visibility into the process of how things are actually done. This helps in the understanding of optimizations and debugging.

If we learn to program in the language c, for example, we can take our skills to any computer with a set of c-based tools. If we learn IA-32 assembly language, we have to relearn a language if we switch to a different architecture.

So, why do we learn assembly language? Because it gives us insight into the underlying hardware, how it is organized, and how it operates.

This book is dedicated to the graduate students in Engineering Science at Loyola College, Columbia Campus, who took the course EG-611, "System Integration I, the x86 Architecture and Assembly Language." The course was given to hundreds of students over a span of 15 years by myself and others.

The author's first computer experience was on a Bendix G-20 mainframe, a 32-bit machine, using the Algol language. His first assembly language was on an IBM S/360 mainframe, specifically the Model 67 variant, with virtual memory. He went on to program the Univac 1108 series mainframe (a 1's complement machine), the DEC PDP-8, 9, 10, and 11, the Bendix G-15, the Athena Missile Guidance Computer by Sperry Rand, designed by Seymour Cray, and many more. The idea of a personal computer was, at the time, ludicrous.

Introduction to the Second Edition

Since the first edition of this book was published, quite a few advances have been made in the X86 area. The author has moved on to the ARM architecture for embedded systems. But, there was a need to correct some typos and formatting issues, to clarify some material, and to add some pictures. There is not much new material included, but the concepts and discussions remain valid. A glossary was added. The pictures are the author's or used courtesy of cpushack.com.

Definitions

Definitions are necessary, so we all have the same meaning in mind for the technical terms.

A bit is the smallest unit of binary information. It represents a yes/no, on/off, left/right type of decision. It can be represented in mathematics as the digits zero or one. Any technology that can represent two distinguishable states can represent a bit. Red light/green light, voltage or no voltage, current or no current, light or darkness, north magnetic or south magnetic, etc. We have to be careful to distinguish between the mathematical concept of a bit (one of two possible states) and its implementation.

Also, we don't need to use base-2 for computers, but it matches the implementation in microelectronics fairly well. Early computers (and calculators) used base-10, which we use because we have ten fingers.

The choice of a base number in mathematics will influence how easy or hard it is to manipulate the numbers. If we just want to know that we have 1 sheep, 2 sheep, or many sheep, we don't need very sophisticated math. The ancient Babylonians used a base-60 math, which survives in the way we tell time (seconds, minutes) and describe angles. They also had computers, abacus units designed to handle their representation of numbers. The Romans did not use a positional number system, which is why it is very hard to do long division in Roman numerals.

A positional number system allows us to choose a base number, and use the digit positions to represent different orders of magnitude, even fractions. In Roman numerals, we have a specific symbol for fifty, and that is L. In decimal, we use 50. That is to say, 5 x 10 (the base) plus 0 times 1.

We need to consider the important concept of zero, which was used in early Mesoamerica, China, India, and other places. The Romans had the concept of zero, just not a specific symbol for it. The zero symbol become important in positional notation, to keep the symbols in the right place, not just to indicate that we have no sheep.

We like to use ten as a base, because we have ten fingers. Actually, we can use any number for a base. The bases of interest to use in computing are base-2 and base-16. For microelectronics, the base-2 is used, because the physics of the devices allow for representation and recognition of two different states easily and efficiently. Base-16 is for our convenience (keep telling yourself that).

We like to use base 10 and computers like to use base 2, so we need to discuss how to convert numbers between these bases.

Technological & Economic Impact

Pc's are tools. Pc's and microelectronics are enabling technologies (like fire, and iron working). They are steps along the way in technology development that enable us to do things easier of faster than we could do before, or to do things we could not do before. They are the building blocks of the technology. In one sense, Pc's feed upon themselves - they are tools to build tools. Modern integrated circuit and software design depend on pc workstations.

Limitations of the technology

The microelectronic used in pc's has some basic limitations imposed by the laws of physics. The speed of light (186,000 miles per second, or 300,000 kilometers per second) sets an upper limit to how fast we can communicate. No information flows faster than the speed of light. System complexity and testability sets limits to the complexity of systems.
Quantum effects become important, as we use smaller and smaller features.

The basis of microelectronic technology is clean sand, silicon being the semiconductor material of choice. It is cheap and plentiful. We use etched 2-dimensional structures to define the devices. Most are made by photochemical means. We don't have practical (i.e., cheap) 3-dimensional structures that are manufacture-able (yet).

Microprocessor chips generate heat when switching, or changing state. This is a tiny amount, but there are millions and hundreds of millions of transistor switches, so the chip-level heat generation get beyond 100 watts. This represents a cooling problem, requiring fans. More importantly, silicon is a poor heat conductor, and small scale features inside the chip may get close to melting temperature due to restricted heat conductance. This has limited chip switching speeds. The use of different substrates can help alleviate the thermal problem. For example, diamond is an excellent thermal conductor, although somewhat pricey.

Planck's constant gives the minimum time to flip a bit = Planck's constant / 4 x E, where E is the Entropy (number of distinguishable states). In binary, E = 2.

And then there's Moore's Law. In 1965, Gordon Moore of Intel observed that the number of transistors per area on integrated circuits doubled every 18 months. It continues to do so. For how long? Moore's law is more of an observation, not a law. It comments on our ability, not our limits. It is an exponential growth law, and there are multiple laws, one for computing, one for memory, one for communication or I/O chips (at least). Exponential growth is not sustainable in the long run.

Number Systems

An important issue in computing is the choice of a base for the number system. We do base 10 because we have 10 fingers. Digital computers, with on/off switching elements, do base 2 mathematics. Actually, any base will work. We like to use base-10, but we could as easily use binary on our 10 fingers to represent quantities up to 1023 (without taking off our shoes). Our current microelectronics technology supports base 2. Mechanical calculators and computers can support base 10

Symbols in the binary system are 0 and 1.These can be represented by on/off, +12/-12 volts, n-magnetic/s-magnetic, whatever physical phenomenon has two states.

A byte is a collection of 8 bits. This makes for a handy size. In binary, a byte can represent 1 of 256 (2^8) possible states or values.

A computer word is a collection of 8, 16, 24, 13, 97, or some other number of bits. The number of bits collected into a word does not need to be a power of two. The range of numbers we can represent depends on how many bits we have in the word. This determines the complexity of the implementation.

A computer performs arithmetic and logic functions on data, and provides flow of control. Let's take these one at a time. The arithmetic functions we would like to have performed are additional, subtraction, multiplication, and division. Actually, as we will see later, if we can subtract, we can do any of these operations. Multiplication is merely repeated addition. The logical operations on binary data include inversion, AND, OR, Exclusive OR, and derivative functions such as Negated-AND (NAND), Negated-OR (NOR), and Negated-Exclusive OR (NXOR). Actually, for two binary symbols, there are 16 possible functions. Only some of these have names (and are useful). As with the mathematical functions, some can be represented as combinations of others. We'll look at mathematical and logical functions applied to binary data, and how the mathematical functions can be expressed in terms of the logical ones.

Computer

Computers do not need to be digital. It's just that we have developed a really good microelectronics capability that implements digital. Mechanical computers and calculators work, although more slowly. Slide rules got us to the moon.

The Von Neumann Architecture says there is no distinction between the code and the data. This was an observation by John Von Neumann of the Institute for Advanced Studies at Princeton University. While consulting for the Moore School of Electrical Engineering at the University of Pennsylvania, Von Neumann wrote an incomplete "First Draft of a Report on the EDVAC" (computer). The paper described a computer architecture in which the data and the program are both stored in the computer's memory in the same address space. Before this, it was the custom to have separate code and data storage (Harvard architecture), and they were not necessarily the same size or format. Von Neumann noted that the code is data. Most modern microprocessors are this style. For speed, especially in digital signal processors, designers revert to the older "Harvard" architecture, with separate code and data stores, as this gives a speed-up in accessing from memory. In a Harvard architecture it is also difficult to have self-modifying code, which is a good thing from the debugging standpoint.

Instruction Set Architecture

The Instruction Set Architecture (ISA) defines the data types, the instructions, the internal architecture of the cpu, addressing modes, interrupt handling, and input/output. The ISA is defined before implementation of the hardware. It may be legacy, as is the case with the Intel 16-bit ISA, now extended to 64 bit, or the ARM ISA. Many other examples can be found in the computer field, such as the Digital Equipment Corporation VAX, and the IBM System/360.

The ISA defines what the processor does, not how it does it. There are different implementations of the ISA that produce the same results with different methods.

The ISA can be emulated or simulated on another machine. Hardware does not need to exist to run an ISA. The Java virtual machine (JVM) was not intended to be instantiated in hardware, but was later implemented in hardware as an exercise.

Data type definitions are part of the ISA. The available data types might include bits, nibbles, BCD, bytes, 16- 32- and 64- bit words, complex number pairs, floating point, double-precision floating point, pixels, etc. Now, the choice of binary over decimal is clear, as binary has the edge in implementation with current state-of-the-art microelectronics. When Babbage designed his difference engine in the 1840's, decimal seemed the better choice. This was partially due to the fact that George Boole had not yet formulated his algebra, to prove how logic functions could implement arithmetic ones.

Instruction types in an ISA include data movement and operations on data. Data movement includes operations to input and output data from external devices, move data to and from registers, and to and from memory. Operations on data include the standard mathematical and logical operations. Control flow instructions provide a mechanism for the independent and data-dependent transfer of control. This group includes branches, jumps, loops, subroutine call and return, interrupt vectoring, and system calls.

The instructions can provide additional features, such as block moves, stack operations, or an atomic test and set. This latter instruction helps implementing coordination among multiple processes, using a mutual exclusion property.

Instruction sets can also have complex entities to implement digital signal processing functions on data, or SIMD (single instruction – multiple data) constructs for vector data processing.

Instructions can have fixed or variable length. Fixed length instructions are easier to pipeline. We can specify multiple operations within one instruction word, allowing more instructions to be fetched at one time. This is the basis for the very long instruction word (VLIW) architecture.

The instruction set can be rich and redundant (complex instruction set - CISC) or reduced (reduced instruction set computer (RISC). In the limit, we might have a one instruction set computer (OISC), a zero instruction set computer (ZISC), or a no instruction set computer (ZISC), which are interesting academic abstractions.

An instruction consists of several parts, the op code, and the operands. The op code is usually the leftmost part of the instruction, the first to be fetched, and thus allowing for the decoding process to begin as the operands are fetched. There may be zero, one, two, three, or more operands. The standard logical or mathematical operation is a function of two (input) variables, and produces a single output.

Output = function (input1, input2)

A standard number of operands, then, would be three. We can reduce this to two, if one of the input operands is also used as the output. If our data structures allows, we might have implied, or zero, operands. This would be the case in a stack architecture, where all the action takes place at the top of the stack. When we say "ADD" the operand at the top of the stack is added to the next operand on the stack, and the result is put on the top of the stack. In a VLIW architecture, we may have multiple sets of op codes and operands in a single instruction word.

Implementation of the instruction set can take many forms. The instruction decoding can be hardwired, or table-driven. Hardwired instruction decoding is fast, but not flexible or changeable. Table-driven allows for the possibility of additions to the instruction set. An ISA can also be implemented in software emulator, which is a computer program that lets a computer of a certain architecture pretend to be something else.

Prefixes

These are standard metric system (SI) prefixes used to represent orders of magnitude in decimal. The same prefixes are used to designate binary powers, but are not part of the SI system.

The prefixes are defined for decimal values, but are also applied to binary numbers. The percent difference is not much, but in the larger magnitudes, can be significant. When someone in the computer or communications industry quotes you a number of gigs-something, stop them and ask if that is decimal or binary.

Generally, memory size is measured in the powers of two, and communication speed measured in decimal powers. Hard disk sizes are specified in decimal units. Clock frequencies are usually specified in decimal. For your convenience.

Prefix	Decimal	Binary	deviation
K = kilo	10^3	2^{10}	2.4%
M = mega	10^6	2^{20}	4.9%
G = gigs	10^9	2^{30}	7.4%
T = tear	10^{12}	2^{40}	10%
P = peat	10^{15}	2^{50}	12.6%
E = exa	10^{18}	2^{60}	15.3%

To date, there have been no reported major failures related to misinterpreting or confusion over units. There have been class action lawsuits regarding confusing information on packaging.

Position notation

In a positional number system, the same symbols are used in different positions to represent multiples of the powers of the base. It is a system for representing numbers by symbols. An alternative, such as Roman numerals, is not a positional system, with unique symbols for different values. Our "Arabic" decimal number system is positional. The Babylonians used a positional number system with base 60. The Maya used base 20.

A number system of a certain base, N, needs N symbols. At the right hand side of our decimal numbers, we have a "decimal point." This separates the positive from the negative powers of the base (i.e., fractions). Similarly, we can have an octal point or a hexadecimal point or a binary point. By convention, digits to the left represent high values of the base.

The decimal systems uses ten unique symbols to represent quantities (0,1,2,3,4,5,6,7,8,9). The binary system uses two (0, 1). Hexadecimal has 16 symbols.

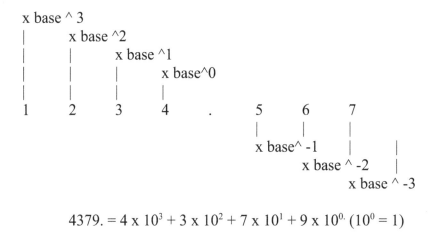

$$4379. = 4 \times 10^3 + 3 \times 10^2 + 7 \times 10^1 + 9 \times 10^0 \; (10^0 = 1)$$

Infinities, overflows, and underflows

Infinity is the largest number that can be represented in the number system. Adding 1 to infinity results in infinity, by definition. In a closed number system imposed by the finite word size of the computer, adding one to infinity results in an overflow, a change of sign.

Negative infinity is the most negative number that can be represented in the number system, not the smallest number.

The least positive number, or the smallest amount that can be represented in the finite number systems is 1. That is because the numbers are usually considered integers, with the binary point on the right of the word. In floating point representation it is different; this will be discussed in the floating point section.

Overflow is the condition in a finite word size machine, where the result of an arithmetic operation is too large to fit in the register. For example, when adding two of the largest positive numbers in a 16-bit representation, the result would not fit in 16 bits. With the use of a two's complement representation scheme for negative numbers, the overflow would result in a sign change, from a large positive to a small negative number.

Overflows can be a problem, as the one that caused the premature termination of the Ariane 5 launch vehicle flight 501. The lost payload was worth more than $300 million.

Underflow is a condition where, as the result of an arithmetic operation, the result is smaller in value than the smallest representable number. The result will be reported as zero in integer representation, even if it is positive, greater than zero, but less than 1. The resolution of binary integers is 1.

Hexadecimal numbers

Hexadecimal (Hex) is a positional number system using base 16. It is a way of grouping four consecutive binary digits into something that looks like a decimal symbol to us humans. Earlier, the octal or base 8 system was used, but this has fell from favor. The idea behind the concept of grouping is that we humans find it difficult to work with very long strings of symbols.

To form a hex number, we group binary digits in 4's. The base is 16. For our decimal numbers, we have 10 symbols, so we will need some more for hex – 6 more. These are the hex symbols for the first 16 numbers: 0,1,2,3,4,5,6,7,8,9,A,B,C,D,E,F. They seem a little strange to us, because there are letters mixed in with our numbers. Don't worry, they are all just symbols. The computer doesn't care - it uses binary.

Hex is also a positional number system, but here, the position indicates a power of 16.

$16^0 = 1$
$16^1 = 16$

$16^2 = 256$
$16^3 = 4096$, etc.

There are also numbers to the right of the hexadecimal point, for quantities that are smaller.

$16^{-1} = 1/16$
$16^{-2} = 1/256$
$16^{-3} = 1/4096$

Elementary Math operations

The elementary math operations include add, subtract, multiply, divide.

The laws of binary addition

0+0=0
1+0=1
0+1=1
1+1=0 (with a carry)

Laws of binary subtraction (Remember a-b does not equal b-a)

0-0=0
0-1=1 (with a borrow)
1-0=1
1-1=0

Laws of binary multiplication

0 x 0 = 0
0 x 1 = 0
1 x 0 = 0
1 x 1 = 1

(that's easy; anything times 0 is 0)

Laws of binary division

(Division by zero is not defined. There is no answer.)

0 / 0 = not allowed
1 / 0 = not allowed
0 / 1 = 0
1 / 1 = 1

Base conversion

Conversion between bases is fairly simple, but has to be learned by practice, just like the laws of mathematics. Most calculators can do it, but it is a useful skill to master. Some day you may find yourself on a deserted island without a calculator.

To go from hex to decimal is a simple algorithm. In mathematics, an algorithm is a method, expressed as a list of well-defined instructions for calculating a function. We can have an algorithm for baking a cake, or calculating conversion between bases.

The key to our conversion algorithm is that both systems are positional, on for base 16 and one for base 10. To see the correspondences between the symbols, A=10, B=11, C=12, D=13, E=14, F=15.

As an example, $13B7_{16}$ equals:

```
1 x 4096 = 4096
3 x 256  =  768
B x 16   =  176 (11x16)
7 x 1    =    7
             5047₁₀
```

The conversion from decimal to hex is a little more complicated. We have to apply successive divisions of powers of the base, saving the remainder for the next step.

What is 943_{10} in hex?

First, 4096 < 943 < 256, so, 943 will have 3 hex digits. More than 2, less than 4.

Then the successive divisions:

```
943 / 256 = 3 remainder 175
175/ 16 = 10 remainder 15
15 / 1 = 15 remainder 0
```

$3/10/15_{10} = 3AF_{16}$

So, what if we see a number like 8A7? We could guess it is hex, because it has one of those hex characters included. But if we saw 894, we really wouldn't know. It is a valid hex and a valid decimal value. When in doubt, indicate the base by a subscript.

Logical operations on data

Logical operations are done on a bit-by-bit basis. There is no interaction between adjacent bit positions.

The Unary function, (function of 1 variable) is "negate". This changes a 0 to a 1, or a 1 to a 0. there is one input, and one output.

There are 16 possible binary functions (function of 2 input variables). These include AND, OR, and XOR, and their negations, NAND, NOR, and NXOR. The other 10 don't have specific names.

$$C = f(A,B)$$

Here is a list of the 16 possible binary functions of 2 inputs. The function designations are mine.

A	B	f1	f2	f3	f4	f5	f6	f7	f8	f9	f10	f11	f12	f13	f14	f15	f16
0	0	0	1	0	1	0	1	0	1	0	1	0	1	0	1	0	1
0	1	0	0	1	1	0	0	1	1	0	0	1	1	0	0	1	1
1	0	0	0	0	0	1	1	1	1	0	0	0	0	1	1	1	1
1	1	0	0	0	0	0	0	0	0	1	1	1	1	1	1	1	1

Where, f2 = NOR, f7=XOR, f8 = NAND, f9=AND, f10=NXOR, and f15=OR.

23

Math in terms of logic functions

Here, we see that mathematical functions can be implemented by logical operations. That's good, because microelectronics implements logical functions easily. George Boole worked out the theoretical basis of this in the middle 1800's.

Addition

+		half-add	carry	
0	0	0	0	$0 + 0 = 0$
0	1	1	0	$0 + 1 = 1$
1	0	1	0	$1 + 0 = 1$
1	1	0	1	$1 + 1 = 0$, with a carry (this is like saying, 5

$+ 5 = 0$,

with a carry, in the decimal

system)

ADD = half-add (XOR) plus carry (AND)

Similarly, for subtraction

-		half-add	borrow	
0	0	0	0	$0 - 0 = 0$
0	1	1	1	$0 - 1 = 0$, with a borrow
1	0	1	0	$1 - 0 = 0$
1	1	0	0	$1 - 1 = 0$

SUB = half-add (XOR) plus borrow (one of the unnamed functions)

We can see that mathematics in the binary system can be implemented with logical functions.

X (times)			multiply
0	0	0	$0 \times 0 = 0$
0	1	0	$0 \times 1 = 0$
1	0	0	$1 \times 0 = 0$
1	1	1	$1 \times 1 = 1$

Multiplication is the AND function.

Division

/

0	0	not allowed	0/0 = not an allowed operation
0	1	0	0/1 = 0
1	0	not allowed	1/0 = not an allowed operation
1	1	1	1/1 = 1

Division is another of the unnamed operations.

Negative numbers

There are many ways to do represent negative numbers. The case we are familiar with from our use of decimal is the use of a special symbol "-". This gives us the sign-magnitude format.

We could do this in binary as well, and, in addition, there are the 1's complement and 2's complement schemes of representing negative numbers. To form the 1's complement of a binary number, change all bits to their logical complement. Problem is, in a finite (closed) number system, the 1's complement system gives two different representations of zero (i.e., +0 and -0), both valid. To form the 2's complement, do the 1's complement and add 1. This is a more complex operation, but the advantage is, there is only one representation of zero. Because zero is considered a positive number, there is one more negative number than positive number in this representation. Two's complement has become the dominant choice for negative number representation in computers.

One's complement was used on the Univac 1108 series mainframes. A problem was that 0 and -0 did not test equal. That can be a problem.

The analog to the complements in the decimal system is 9's complement and 10's complement, but these are not taught any more, and don't get used much.

Subtraction

Subtraction can be accomplished by addition of the complement. We don't need a separate subtract-er circuit. We can use the adder, and we need a complement (inverter) circuit, which is easy. Logical operations such as complement operate on a bit-by-bit basis with no "carry" or "borrow" from adjacent bits, like we would find in mathematical operations.

Subtraction example

-	0	1		b	0	1		b=borrow
0	0	1		0	0	0		
1	1	0		1	1	0		

Remember a-b does not equal b-a. Subtraction depends on the order of the operands.

In hex,

E 8 h ->	1110 1000
-5 A h →	0101 1010
8 E h →	1000 1110

Add 2's complement:

$$5 A h = 0101\ 1010$$
$$1's\ comp = 1010\ 0101\ (A5h)$$
$$2's\ comp = 1010\ 0110\ (A6h)$$

E 8 h -> 1110 1000
+ A 6 h -> 1010 0110
1 8 E h   110001110 ignore overflow

If division is equivalent to repeated subtraction, and subtraction is the same as the addition of the complement, and multiplication is repeated addition, then all we really need is an addition circuit, and a complementer. Since addition can be accomplished by the logic circuits AND and XOR, we can in theory implement all binary mathematical operations in terms of logic functions. That's the theory. It works. There's better ways to do it.

Multiplication

Multiplication by digit is possible, but can take excessive time, with long digits. The multiplication table in binary is rather simple, though. Only one of four cases results in an non-zero result. The multiplication of two n-bit numbers requires n^2 operations. The results for a multiplication of two n-bit numbers can be 2n bits wide.

Shift-and-add is a common multiplication technique in binary. Shifting gives us successive powers of two. There do exist special algorithms for multiplication and division, so we don't need to do repeated adds or subtracts. Examples are the Karatsuba method, and the Toom-Cook algorithm. We can also design a digital multiplier for hexadecimal numbers, so we do 4 binary digits per clock. This can make use of a look-up table.

Multiplication of fractions takes the form of normal multiplication, with due diligence of the resulting binary point.

In optimizing integer multiplications, we can speed up the process where we have a variable times a constant. First, if the constant is a power of two, the multiplication can be accomplished with shifts. Similarly, multiplication by sums of powers of two is also easily handled (i.e., 6 = 4+2, 10 = 8+2). With a bit more work, we can factor the fixed multiplicand into powers of two (i.e., 13 = 8 + 4 + 1; 15 = 16 - 1) and accomplish the multiplication with shifts and adds. This works for fairly complex numbers, because the cost of a multiply instruction is high, whereas the shifts, adds, and subtracts are usually optimized to be single clock operations. This technique requires knowledge of the individual instruction times.

Division is a big, ugly, and time-consuming operation, to be avoided whenever possible. The division operation is usually the slowest one in the instruction set. This sets a lower limit to interrupt latency in real-time systems, and can certainly effect system throughput.

A special case, of division is the reciprocal, 1/X. Here, the numerator of the fraction is known, and the division easier. After forming the reciprocal, which takes less time than an arbitrary division, a multiplication is required.

$$A/B = A \times (1/B)$$

In integer multiplication, division of a value by a power of two can be accomplished by shifts.

Data structures

The structure and organization of your data can have more of an impact on program size and execution time than your algorithm. Think through the data organization, to simplify the processing. Put your initial effort into the definition of the data structures, and the algorithm will fall out.

Integers

All the numbers we talk about will be integers (until we get to floating point). Integers have a finite range. Eight bits gives us 256 (2^8) numbers, and 16 bits gives us nearly 65000. We need to give up one bit (or, 1/2 of our range of numbers) for a sign position.

BCD Format

Binary Coded Decimal uses 10 of the possible 16 codes in 4 bits. The other bit patterns are not used, or could be used to indicate sign, error, overflow, or such. BCD converts to decimal easily, and provides a precise representation of decimal numbers. It requires serial by digit calculations, but gives exact results. It uses more storage than binary integers, and the implementation of the logic for operations is a bit more complex. It is an alternative to the limited range or precision of binary integers, and the complexity of floating point. BCD is used extensively in instrumentation and personal calculators. Support for operations on BCD numbers were provided in the IBM mainframes, and the Intel x86 series of microprocessors.

BCD 4 bit code, only 10 valid values:

0000 = 0	0001 = 1	0010 = 2	0011 = 3	0100 = 4
0101 = 5	0110 = 6	0111 = 7	1000 = 8	1001 = 9

1010, 1011, 1100, 1101, 1110, 1111 = invalid number codes in BCD

BCD numbers (4 bits) can be stored in a byte, which uses more storage, but makes calculations easier. These are sometimes referred to as BCD nibbles. Alternately, BCD digits can be packed 2 to a byte.

Arithmetic operations in BCD format numbers are usually done in binary, and then adjusted to handle the carry (or borrow). For example, in packed BCD, we may generate a carry between the 3rd and 4th bit position. Subtraction is usually implemented by adding the 10's complement of the subtrahend. The 10's complement is formed by taking the 9's complement, and then adding one. The 9's complement can be formed by subtracting the digits from 9. If a BCD arithmetic operation generates an invalid BCD result, 6 can be added to force a carry. BCD strings of numbers can have a "decimal point" inserted wherever convenient. Additional bookkeeping is then needed to keep the numbers commensurate for addition and subtraction, and to adjust in multiplication and division.

ASCII Format

American Standard Code for Information Interchange (ASCII) was devised for communication of symbols for teletypes from the 1960's. It is a 7-bit code with 128 combinations. This gives us four groups of 32: control, lower case, upper case, numbers and punctuation characters. An ASCII character fits in an 8-bit byte, with one bit to spare. This is sometimes used as a parity bit, for error control. At the time, paper tape systems supported 8 bits. Later, support was included in 9-track, reel-to-reel tape and punch cards.

Although a 7-bit code can handle the Roman alphabet, upper and lower case, numbers, punctuation, and control characters, it is not useful for character systems (such as Amharic) that have a large number of letter combinations, or logosyllabic systems such as Chinese. ASCII extensions address variations in Latin letters, such as those found in Italian, Spanish, Portuguese, French, and other Latin based languages, and regional uses, such as the British Pound sign (for currency), represented on US keyboards as "#".

Earlier codes, such as the 5-bit Baudot code (circa 1870), used a *shift* mechanism to allow additional codes. The term "baud," referring to the symbol rate of transmission of information, is named for Emile Baudot, the originator of the code. Baud rate is not necessarily the same as bit rate; it depends on how many bits it takes to represent a symbol (such as a Baudot or ASCII character). Baudot code was used well into the 20th century for teleprinter equipment, particularly on the AT&T TWX network.

An Escape sequence is initiated by a special code, the Escape character (ESC). This defines the following characters to be control characters, not encoded numbers or digits, until a second ESC is received. This is contrasted with control characters, that have defined functions, such as tab or carriage return (which is a typewriter term). The ESC key is still included on keyboards. Control characters usually have no displayed equivalent.

ASCII's heritage in teletype machines sometimes causes confusion in modern data communications. For example, teletypes needed both a carriage return (CR) and a line feed (LF) at the end of a line. Non-mechanical systems can do both operations with just a CR. The Bell character, designed to ring the Teletype's bell at the receiving end for attention (or annoyance) has no parallels. The Backspace character was used to back up paper tape to overwrite errors. ASCII is defined to be transmitted least significant bit first.

Parity

Parity is a simple error control mechanism for communications and storage. We add an extra bit to the word, so we can adjust parity. Parity is based on the mathematical concept of even (evenly divisible by two) or odd. In binary, a number is even if its least-significant (rightmost) digit is zero (0).

For example, in ASCII,

$A = 41_{16} = 0100\ 0001 = 2\ (1's) = even$
$B = 42_{16} = 0100\ 0010 = 2\ (1's) = even$
$C = 43_{16} = 0100\ 0011 = 3\ (1's) = odd$

If we want to always have even parity, we would make the extra bit = 0 for A & B, 1 for C, etc.

Here is an algorithm for parity calculation: Count the number of 1 bits in a word. If the count is odd, the word has odd parity. If the count is even, the word has (you guessed it) even parity. If we're going to communicate or store the word, we agree ahead of time it has a certain parity. If we see a different parity, there is an error. If we see the correct parity, the word is good, or it has multiple errors. Multiple errors are usually less likely than single errors, so the mechanism works somewhat well. The overhead is one extra bit.

If we want to get fancy, there are other schemes that use multiple bits to allow detection, and even correction, of multiple bit errors. These EDC (Error Detecting and Correction) codes are outside the scope of our discussion, but are widely use in data storage and communication.

Lists

Lists are one of many data structures we can define in memory. Then we can store data into them, and process it as we wish. Some forms of lists are particularly useful.

Consecutive lists can be made with bytes, words, or doublewords. The list is just an abstraction that we use. The data items are stored in adjacent memory locations in the physical memory. We need to mark end of list with a special character (EOF, end of file), or keep count of number of entries in the list.

Lists can be ordered or non-ordered. In a non-ordered list, adjacent elements have no particular relationship to their neighbors, except for being members of the same list. To add an element into a non-ordered list, we just store it at end of the list, then update the element count or move the EOF. To delete an element, we delete it, move subsequent elements up to close the gap, then update count or move the EOF. Alternately, we can mark the element as deleted, don't bother moving other elements; and go back later and clean up. This process is called garbage collection.

To search for an element, we need to examine each item, starting from first item, until the match is found.

With an ordered list, where elements do have a relationship with their neighbors, we can take advantage of that relationship to make adding, deleting, or searching faster. We might, for example, sort the data in ascending or descending order as it is inserted. This makes insertion of a new data item a longer process, because we have to figure out where in the list it belongs, but it makes searching much faster. Do we do more inserting or searching?

A bubble sort is a search algorithm over an ordered list; a binary search for example. We first check whether the item would be in the first half or the second half of the list. We can do this because the list is ordered. Then we search the first or second half of the selected half, etc., eliminating half of the remaining search space on each iteration, until we get a single result. The result bubbles up.

To add an element to an ordered list, we need to find out where it should go, move other elements to make room, insert it, and update the element count or move the EOF as applicable. To delete an element from an ordered list, we need to find the element, delete it, move elements up to close the gap, update the count or move the EOF. Alternately, we can mark it as deleted, don't move the other elements; and garbage collect later. Garbage collection is the process of getting rid of unused data. It is actually recycling. We can reuse the bits, and the memory space. If we don't do garbage collection, the list just keeps getting bigger, and we can have a condition called a memory leak, where we run out of available memory.

Items in linked lists are not necessarily stored consecutively in adjacent memory locations. Each element of the list has two parts: the data itself, and a link to the next item. We can have both forward and backward links. A linked list can be ordered or non-ordered; all the previous discussions apply. The first entry in the list can be the length of the list. The last element of the list can have a null link.

Look up Tables

If memory is a less valuable resource than processing time, we might decide to pre-compute items and store them in a look-up table. This works well with complex calculations; we only do them once, and offline. Example items might include sine, cosine, exponential, complex logarithmic functions, and such. We can also simplify the table by exploiting symmetries in the function.

Jump tables are tables of addresses, for changes in the flow of control. The interrupt mechanism uses a table of jump addresses, indexed by the interrupt number, to vector to an associated interrupt handler routine in a short time.

A stack is a first-in, last-out data structure. It can be implemented in random access memory. Accessing items on the stack doesn't need an explicit address; the action happens on the top of the stack. A stack is referred to as a zero-address structure. The IA-86 supports stack operations.

Hardware Elements of a Computer

This section will discuss the hardware components of a computer, specifically that of the Intel x86 family. Starting in 1978, Intel introduced the 16-bit 8086 as a follow-on to the 8-bit 8080 processor. The family continues today, almost 35 years later. It retains the same basic architecture as the earliest chips, and so constitutes a valid family of devices.

The newer devices are 64-bit, and nearly a thousand times faster.

<u>80x86 family pedigree</u>

 8086 16-bit processor, circa 1978. addresses 1 megabyte; 6-byte instruction queue, 6 MHz

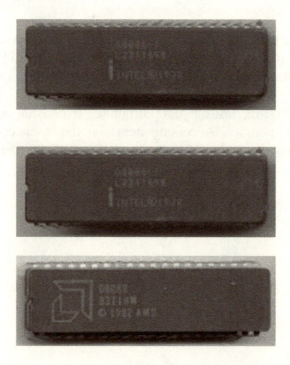

 8088   8-bit external bus version of 8086. chosen by IBM to be the basis for the pc; 4 byte instruction queue

80186   advanced features integrated on-chip

80188   8-bit external bus interface version of 80186

80286   chosen by IBM to be basis of AT machines

80386 announced 1985, generally available 1987. True 32-bit architecture with multitasking support.

386 in flatpack configuration. Set yo be soldered on a board, not in a socket.

80386sx   16-bit external bus version of 80386.

The 80386EX was an embedded variation of the 386 architecture, with included I/O.

The 80486 was announced 1988, available 1989, 25, 33, 50 MHz, reported to be 4 times faster than 80386 at same clock speed due to internal speed up of operations.

The 80586, common name, Pentium, 5th generation chip, 1993.

Beyond this are the Pentium-Pro, Pentium-II, Pentium III, Pentium 4, Atom, and more advanced architectures with multiple cores. We'll stop this discussion at the moment with the Pentium. We will discuss the architecture in three sections, the CPU, I/O, and Memory. All computers have these three elements.

The Central Processing Unit

A computer performs arithmetic and logic functions on data, and provides flow of control. Let's take these one at a time. The arithmetic functions we would like to have performed are additional, subtraction, multiplication, and division. Actually, as we will see later, if we can subtract, we can do any of these operations. The logical operations on binary data include inversion, AND, OR, Exclusive OR, and derivative functions such as Negated-AND (NAND), Negated-OR (NOR), and Negated-Exclusive OR (NXOR). As with the mathematical functions, some can be represented as combinations of others. We look at mathematical and logical functions applied to binary data, and how the mathematical functions can be expressed in terms of the logical ones.

40

The fetch/execute cycle

This section discusses how an instruction gets executed. The basic process is referred to as the fetch/execute cycle. First the instruction is fetched from memory, then the instruction is executed, which can involve the fetching and writing of data items, as well as mathematical and logical operations on the data.

Instructions are executed in steps called machine cycles. Each machine cycle might take several machine clock times to complete. If the architecture is pipelined, then each machine cycle consists of a stage in the pipeline. At each step, a memory access or an internal operation (ALU operation) is performed. Machine cycles are sequenced by a state machine in the cpu logic. A clock signal keeps everything going in lockstep.

A register called the program counter holds a pointer to the location in memory of the next instruction to be executed. At initialization (boot), the program counter is loaded with the location of the first instruction to be executed. After that, the program counter is simply incremented, unless there is a change in the flow of control, such as a branch or jump. In this case, the target address of the branch or jump is put into the program counter.

The first step of the instruction execution is to fetch the instruction from memory. It goes into a special holding location called the Instruction Register. At this point the instruction is decoded, meaning a control unit figures out, from the bit pattern, what the instruction is to do. This control unit implements the ISA, the instruction set architecture. Without getting too complicated, we could have a flexible control unit that could execute different ISA's. That's possible, but beyond the scope of our discussion here.

The instruction decode complete, the machine knows what resources are required for instruction execution. A typical math instruction, for example, would require two data reads from memory, an ALU operation, and a data write. The data items might be in registers, or memory. If the instruction stream is regular, we can pipeline the operation. We have stages in the pipeline for instruction fetch, instruction decode, operand(s) read, ALU operation, and operand write. If we have a long string of math operations, at some point, each stage in the pipeline is busy, and an instruction is

41

completed at each clock cycle. But, if a particular instruction requires the result of a previous instruction as an input, the scheme falls apart, and the pipeline stalls. This is called a dependency, and can be addressed by the compiler optimizing the code by re-ordering. This doesn't always work. When a change in the flow of control occurs (branch, jump, interrupt), the pipeline has to be flushed out and refilled. On the average, the pipeline speeds up the process of executing instructions.

A special purpose hardware device, purpose-built, will always be faster than a general purpose device programmed or configured for a specific task. This means that purpose-built hardware is the best, yet least flexible choice. Programmability provides flexibility, and reduces the cost of change. A new approach, provided by Field Programmable Gate Array (FPGA) technology, gives us the ability to reconfigure the hardware and well as the software. That discussion is beyond the scope of this book.

The optimization might be in a different data type, floating point, or vector data as opposed to integers, or in the types of operations required.

Besides the integer processor, we can have a specialized floating point unit (FPU), that operands on floating point operands. It can have its own pipeline to expedite execution.

Support Chips for 80x86

The early members of the x86 family were just cpu's. Other functions such as interrupt or video handling were relegated to support chips. As technology advances permitted, some of these functions were included on the cpu chip, or combined into one large chip. The IBM pc architecture drove board level designs, and several vendors produce complex chips, that combined with the cpu and memory, to implement an IBM pc. It is important to recognize what functions are defined by the x86 cpu architecture, and which are defined by design decisions at the board level. Chip functions will be the same for any device using that chip. Designers are free to build their board any way they like, with additional functional definitions. One standard in this area is the IBM pc, personal computer architecture. Individual chips for many additional functions can be found on older boards. The legacy functions are provided in the new hardware designs. The IBM pc also includes an 8-bit data bus (Industry Standard Architecture - ISA) for accessory cards, and the IBM AT provides a 16-bit bus (Extended ISA - EISA). Now we have the 32-bit PCI bus and follow-ons to that.

The 8259 chip from Intel was an interrupt controller, providing prioritization and 8 levels of interrupt. The chip is chain-able. One is used in the IBM pc design for 8 levels of interrupt, and two are used in the IBM AT for 15 levels. This chip provides the interface between interrupting devices and the cpu.

The Intel 8237 is a DMA (Direct Memory Access) controller. It provides the handshaking with 4 external dma channels. The pc architecture uses one, and the AT architecture uses two, for 8 channels. DMA is typically used for fast transfer devices such as disks and networks. In the pc architecture, the dynamic refresh function is handled as a type of DMA protocol.

The Intel 8284 is a Clock Generator chip, which provides the multiphase clock generation for the cpu, and reset synchronization. Originally, the IBM pc used a clock frequency of 4.77 MHz, with 6 MHz capable parts. This was because a single crystal was used for the cpu clock, and the video display.

14.3128 / 3 = 4.77 MHz for cpu; and
14.3128 / 4 = 3.578 MHz = color burst signal for the video display.

The Intel 8255 chip is a triple 8-bit parallel port. The 8253 is a Programmable timer for the pc. The follow-on 8254 is a Programmable timer for the AT. These timers were used for sound generation, the cassette I/O functions, and the real-time clock.

A non-Intel part, the Motorola 6845 chip, was used as a CRT Video controller in the pc architecture.

 The 765 chip from NEC provided the logic for the Floppy Disk Controller. This was a simple embedded controller that interfaced with and controlled the floppy disk drive.

Later, the functionality of these parts was incorporated into 1 or 2 large gate arrays, available from multiple vendors. These were defined as the Northbridge and Southbridge, handling memory access and I/O features respectively. We could have 3 chips (cpu, Northbridge, Southbridge) plus memory, rather than hundreds of chips. Now, with the ability to incorporate even more functionality into increasingly complex chips, single-chip pc designs with these functions sharing silicon with the cpu, is becoming common.

X86 Processor family

The 80x86 processor family began with the 8086 and 8088 models in 1978 and 1979. These were extended to the 80286 in 1982. Each of these had an associated floating point coprocessor, the 8087 and 80287. Floating point is discussed in the Appendix. The floating point units are ALU's for this format.

The architecture was extended from 16 bits to 32 with the introduction of the 80386 in 1985, and its associated coprocessor, the 80387. The '386 and its associated coprocessor, were available in 16-bit external bus versions, the SX series. The 80486 in 1989 combined the coprocessor and the main processor on the same chip. In addition, many other companies (such as AMD, NEC, IDT, Texas Instruments, IBM, OKI, Fujitsu, Siemens, and others) also produced these chips and variations under license. The commonality was the ISA-86. The floating point coprocessor for the 80386 was the 80387. The 80486, and subsequent chips, incorporated the floating point unit on the same chip as the integer processor

There were also third-party floating point chips from Weitek, Cyrix, and others.

A chart at the end of this book lists some of the 80x86 members, from the 8086 to the 64-bit Pentium-D.

Numerous companies are represented. The data bus column gives the width of the data bus form 16 bits to today's 64 bits. The address bus column shows the width of the external memory bus. The maximum word size shows the width of internal registers. The number 80 indicates the 80-bit floating point format.

The 8088 was the 8-bit external bus version of the 8086. Each memory word took two accesses. This was to save cost on the memory architecture. The 8088 was chosen by IBM to be the basis of their PC architecture. Embedded control versions of the architecture were introduced as the 80188 and 80186. These included some additional devices on the same chip, to reduce chip count in a system, while maintaining compatibility with the ISA-86.

Around this time, Intel experimented with a 32-bit architecture, the iAPX432, but it didn't amount to much of a commercial product. NEC's V-20 product was interesting. It was a direct plug-in replacement for the 8088, but also had an 8-bit Intel 8080 processor compatibility mode. The V-30 chip did the same for an 8086.

These devices were designed to ease the transition from 8-bit to 16-bit, by allowing legacy code to still run. The 80286 chip introduced Protected Mode, an arrangement to extend the addressing capability beyond 1 megabyte to 16 megabytes. The 80386sx was also introduced with an "8088-like" interface. The 80386sx and 387sx used a 16 bit memory interface. For a while, the 80286 was actually faster at executing instructions than the 80386 (at the same clock rate), but this advantage was rapidly overtaken by increasing clock rates.

The 80386 featured a 32-bit real address, and 32-bit registers. It had a 46-bit virtual address, with an on-chip memory management unit (MMU) to translate virtual to real addresses. There were now 6 instead of 4 segment registers, optional paging support in the MMU, hardware support for multitasking, and some new instructions. The 80386 supported memory management by segmentation in the new Protected mode. The '386 I/O supported 16- and 32-bit I/O using adjacent I/O space byte addresses. The 32-bit flags register was a superset of the 16-bit one, with the lower 16 bits being identical, and new flags in the upper part. There were three new control registers, six debug registers for breakpoint addresses. There were additional registers to support segmentation. The 80386 had three modes of operation. Real mode made it a big strong 8086 with 32 new instructions, 2 new segment registers, and the debug registers.. Virtual-86 mode added MMU functions for paging and a multitasking environment. Protected mode was the big change. The earliest 80386's could use the 80287 math coprocessor, but that changed when the 80387 became available. There were also third-party floating point processor chips that were compatible.

The floating point coprocessor in the Intel architecture executes from the same instruction stream as the main processor. For operand fetch, the coprocessor uses a memory cycle steal, something like a DMA operation as far as the main processor is concerned. The coprocessor has its own set of internal registers, organized as a stack. Registers are 80 bits wide.

The Intel numeric coprocessors do operations on extended precision integer (64-bit) and floating point format. They are faster than the main processor in these operations, and, in addition, operate in parallel with it. For example, a 64x64 bit multiply would takes 2100 microseconds on the 8086, but only 30 microseconds on the 8087 coprocessor, a speed up of a factor of seventy.

The Intel processors and associated coprocessors form a tightly coupled pair. The main processor does all the instruction fetching. In addition, it is responsible for transferring data to the coprocessor's registers. Execution of coprocessor instructions proceeds in parallel with those of general instructions. The coprocessor recognizes its own instructions, and executes them. Coprocessor instructions start with a hex F. The main processor ignores coprocessor instructions. Between the main cpu and the coprocessor, there is a busy/wait handshake mechanism for coordination. There is a control word and a status word in internal registers in the floating point unit. The floating point unit also maintains its own instruction pointer and an operand pointer. The floating point unit can generate exceptions including invalid operation, attempted division by zero, normalized, overflow, underflow, and inexact result.

The instruction set includes load and store; the basic add, subtract, multiply, and divide; compare; square root; and certain pre-calculated constants in floating point format such as zero, one, pi, $log_2(10)$, and others.

The 80486 added the MMU and the floating point functionality inboard the same chip, with a small 8 kilobyte on-chip data and instruction cache. More operations became single cycle, and string operations were made faster. A barrel shifter provided faster shifts. The internal data buses were wider, for faster data transfer. The '486 introduced the Byte Swap instruction to reverse the endianess of data items. This allowed easier access to IBM mainframe and Apple-Motorola data. In addition, if the 80486 tried to access data that was misaligned, an interrupt was generated. This condition is transparent to the running program, but slows it down considerably.

The Intel Pentium, or 5th generation, was matched by the 5x86 from Cyrix, the Nx586 from Nexgen,

and AMD's K5. At this point, executing the ISA-86 was the thread connecting these processors. Their internal structures differed greatly. IDT came out with their C3, C6, and C7, while Intel pursued the Pentium-II and Pentium-III.

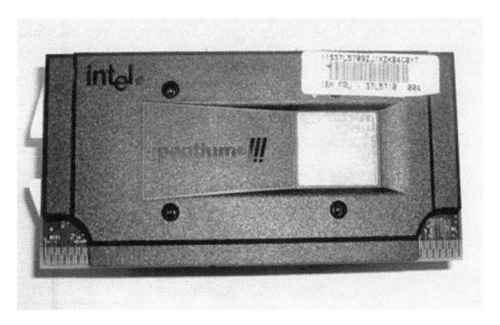

51

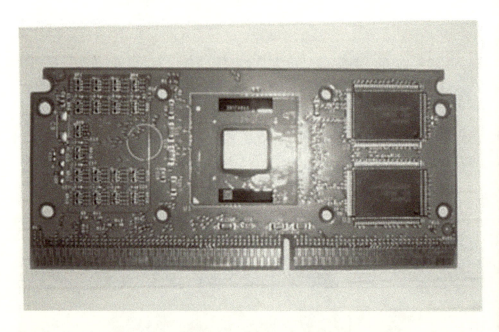

Intel's PentiumPro was targeted to higher-horsepower servers. They had cache die integrated on the same substrate of the processor. AMD introduced their K6 series, and the K7 Athlons and Durons.

AMD K6.

AMD Athlon.

The Intel Pentium 4 and AMD's K8 Opterons appeared next.

Other AMD chips included the Duron and Sempron.

A particularly interesting niche chip was the Transmeta Crusoe of the year 2000. It used a very long instruction word (VLIW) approach, with an X-86 emulator, and just-in-time translation. In addition, other instruction set architectures could also be emulated. The Transmeta chips were designed to be low power, for laptop applications. The second generation chip was the Efficion.

Other x86 implementations that used emulation or translation of X86 instruction to internal RISC (reduced instruction set computer) instructions included NexGen Nx586,

the PowerPC 625, the IMS 6250, the Toshiba R4x00 Tigershark, which translated x86 to MIPS, and others. By the introduction of the Pentium-II and Pentium-III, Intel was also translating x86 to an internal optimized instruction set.

At this point in the technology curve, not only could large amounts of cache memory be included with the cpu chip, but multiple cpu's could be included in one package, a technique referred to as multicore. The Pentium is, essentially a pair of '386's plus a '387. Intel's patented technique of hyperthreading refers to a simultaneous multithreading implementation in Pentium 4 and subsequent processors. Multiple threads of execution are supported. The hardware plus the operating system software operate with two virtual processors per physical cpu core. This approach is transparent to the software. It is not quite as fast as having two physical processor, but is certainly faster than one.

The x86 architecture has been extended to 64 bits, the IA-64. This includes not only 64-bit addresses and data, but significant levels of instruction parallelism, using speculative execution, branch prediction, a register stack, and other optimization techniques. It remains binary compatible with IA-32.

Instruction level parallelism provides an avenue to higher performance, at the cost of complexity. We include additional hardware, with the overhead of managing and coordinating this hardware. One technique is instruction re-ordering at run time, in hardware. This means the hardware examines the instruction flow to recognize and exploit opportunities for parallelism. We can also try to predict branches. Your first guess would be that you would be right ½ the time. For something like a loop structure, you could be right most of the time, if you guessed that the branch was taken. In the control speculation approach, we move loads and their dependencies above branches. In data speculation, we can move loads above possible conflicting memory references. With control flow prediction, we guess, and take the consequences. Unwinding the results of a wrong guess may not incur a large penalty. One approach is to execute down two branch paths simultaneously until the branch is resolved. The correct path is continued, and the incorrect path is discarded.

Input/Output

Input/Output (I/O) provides a user interface, and a link between systems. The basic I/O methods of polled, interrupt, and dma are supported by the cpu chips, but additional support chips are required to implement these functions. There are many options. We will consider the specific implementation of the IBM pc circuit board, which has evolved into an industry standard architecture.

I/O Methods

Regardless how bits or signals come to a computer, there are several standards methods to sample them, or send them out. The various communication protocols define the physical connection (connectors) and electrical interface (voltages, etc.). Once we are at the processor chip boundary, and we are dealing with bits, there are three common schemes to read or write. These can be implemented in hardware or software. The three schemes are polled I/O, interrupts, or direct memory access. All of these schemes work with serial (bit-at-a-time) or parallel (many-bits-at-a-time) I/O.

There are three basic methods for I/O implementation, polled I/O, interrupts, and direct memory access.

Polled I/O

In polled I/O, the computer periodically checks to see if data is available, or if the communications channel is ready to accept new output. This is somewhat like checking your phone every few seconds to see if anyone is calling. There's a more efficient way to do it, which we'll discuss next, but you may not have anything better to do. Polled I/O is the simplest method. Specific I/O instructions are provided in the Intel processors. Both serial and parallel interfaces are used on the IBM pc board level architecture.

Interrupt

In Interrupt I/O, when a new piece of information arrives, or the communication channel is ready to accept new output, a control signal called an interrupt occurs. This is like the phone ringing. You are sitting at your desk, busy at something, and the phone rings, interrupting you, causing you to set aside what you are doing, and handle the new task. When that is done, you go back to what you were doing. A special piece of software called an interrupt service routine is required. At this point, the phone rings....

Control transfer mechanism, somewhat like a subroutine call, but can be triggered by an external event. External events can make a request for service. The Intel cpu architecture supports 256 levels of interrupt, with a single interrupt line. The specific interrupt number is put on the cpu data bus, in the lower 8-bits. This requires one or more external interrupt prioritization chips. The IBM pc architecture uses 8 levels of interrupt, and the later IBM AT architecture supports 15.

Sources for Interrupts

There are hardware interrupts, defined by the architecture of the cpu and the motherboard it resides on. These interrupts are triggered by events external to the cpu, and are thus asynchronous to its operation

We can get the same effect by executing software interrupt commands. This provides a convenient mechanism for a user program to call the Operating System and request services. There interrupts are synchronous.

Exceptions are interrupts caused in response to a condition encountered during execution of an instruction. For example, an attempted division by zero would trigger an exception. These are also synchronous interrupts.

External Interrupts are asynchronous to the CPU's operation. It is hard to duplicate their timing. There are implications for debugging multiple interrupt systems in a real-time environment. We need to know the state of the machine, at every instant of time.

DMA

Direct Memory access is the fastest way to input or output information. It does this directly to or from memory, without processor intervention.

Let's say we want to transmit a series of 32-bit words. The processor would have to fetch this word from memory, send it to the I/O interface, and update a counter. In DMA, the I/O device can interface directly to or from the memory. DMA control hardware includes housekeeping tasks such as keeping a word count, and updating the memory pointer.

DMA also makes use of interrupts. Normally, we load a word count into a register in the DMA controller, and it is counted down as words transfer to or from memory. When the word count reaches zero, and interrupt is triggered to the processor to signal the end of the transfer event.

While the DMA is going on, the processor may be locked out of memory access, depending on the memory architecture. Also, if dynamic memory is being used, the processor is usually in charge of memory refresh. This can be handled by the DMA controller, but someone has to do it.

The DMA scheme used on the IBM pc toggles between the CPU and the DMA device on a per-word basis. Thus, the processor is not locked out of fetching and executing instructions during a DMA, although the DMA transfer is not as fast as it could be.

Also, DMA is not constrained to access memory linearly; that is a function of the DMA controller and its complexity. For example, the DMA controller can be set up to access every fourth word in memory.

The DMA protocol uses a Request and Grant mechanism. The device desiring to use dma send a request to the cpu, and that request is granted when the cpu is able. This is similar to the interrupt request for service mechanism. A dma controller interfaces with the device and the cpu. It may handle multiple dma channels with differing priorities. The controller has to know, for each request, the starting address in memory, and the size of the data movement. For dma data coming in to ram, there is the additional complication of updating cache.

During the dma transfer, the dma controller takes over certain tasks from the cpu. This includes updating the memory address, and keeping track of the word count. The word count normally goes to zero, and generates an interrupt to signal the cpu that the dma transfer is over. The cpu can continue execution, as long as it has code and data available.

DMA on the Intel cpu chips requires an external DMA controller function. Each controller supports 4 channels of dma.

Serial versus parallel

A bus architecture is used as a short-distance parallel communications pathway between functional elements, such as the cpu and memory. The length of parallel signal lines is severely restricted by bit skew, where all the bits don't get to a particular point at the same time. This is due in some part by the differing characteristics of the circuit board traces implementing the bus. Each path must be treated as a transmission line at the frequencies involved, and have balanced characteristics with all the other lines, and be properly terminated.

Serial communication can take place at gigabit rates, and does not suffer from bit skew. In addition, it can take be used over arbitrary distances, and with various carrier schemes. At this moment, the Voyager spacecraft is sending data back to Earth over a serial radio frequency link, even though the spacecraft is outside the solar system, at a nominal 40 bits per second.

A UART, Universal Asynchronous Receiver Transmitter, has industry standard functionality for serial asynchronous communication. An example of the hardware part is the 8251 chip. A UART may also be implemented in software. The functionality includes support for all of the standard formats (bits, parity, and overhead).

Serial communication of multiple bits utilizes time domain multiplexing of the communication channel, as bits are transmitted one at a time.

The serial communication parameters of interest include:
- Baud rate. (Symbol rate)
- Number of bits per character.
- endian – MSB or LSB transmitted first
- Parity/no parity.
- If parity, even or odd.
- Length of a stop bit (1, 1.5, 2 bits)

The baud rate gives the speed of transmission of data characters. The bit rate is the speed of individual bits making up the information and the overhead. For example, if we have 8 data bits and 3 overhead bits, and we transfer characters at 1000 baud, we are using a bit rate of 13000 bits per second.

What is the length of a bit? This is the time period of a bit, the reciprocal of the frequency. At 1000 Hertz, a bit is 1/1000 second, or 1 millisecond long.

In synchronous communication, a shared clock is used between the transmitter and receiver. This clock can be transmitted on a second channel, or be a shared resource, such as GPS-derived time. In synchronous systems, characters are transmitted continuously. If there is no data to transmit, a special SYN character is used.

In asynchronous communication, the transmitter and receiver have their own local clocks, and the receiver must synchronize to the transmitter clock. The receiver and transmitter clocks are usually very accurate, being derived from crystal oscillators. Clock drift between the units is less of a problem than phase – the receiver does not know when a transmission begins. This is accomplished by a shared protocol.

When characters are not being transmitted in an asynchronous scheme, the communications channel is kept at a known idle state, known as a "Mark", from the old time telegraph days. Morse code is binary, and the manual teletypes used the presence or absence of a voltage (or current through the line) to represent one state, and the absence to indicate the other state. Initially, the key press or "1" state was "voltage is applied", and the resting state was no voltage. Since these early systems used acid-filled batteries, there was a desire among operators to extend the battery life, without having to refill the batteries. Problem is, if the wire were cut (maliciously or accidentally), there was no indication. The scheme was changed to where the resting state was voltage on the line. Thus, if the line voltage dropped to zero, there was a problem on the channel.

The digital circuitry uses mostly 5 volts, and the RS-232 standard for serial communication specifies a plus/minus voltage. Usually 12 volts works fine. In any case, interface circuitry at each end of the line convert line voltage to +5/0 volts for the computer circuitry. One state is called "marking" and the other state is called "spacing".

The receiver does bit re-timing on what it receives. Knowing when the transmission started, and the width of the bits, it knows when to sample them and make a choice between one and zero. From communications theory, the best place to sample is in the middle of the bit.

At idle, which is an arbitrary period in asynchronous communication, the input assumes one known state. When it changes to another state, the receiver knows this is the start of a transmission, and the beginning or leading edge of a "start" bit. Since the receiver knows the baud rate a priori, because of an agreement with the transmitter, it waits one bit period to get to the first data bit leading edge, and then an additional one-half bit period to get to the middle of the bit. This is the ideal point (in communications theory terms) to sample the input bit. After, that, the receiver waits one additional bit period to sample the second bit in the center, etc., for the agreed-upon number of bits in a word. Then the receiver samples the parity bit (if the agreement allows for one), and then waits one, one and a half, or two bit periods for the "stop bits". After that, any change in the sensed bit state is the start bit of a new transmission. If the receiver and transmitter use different baud clock, the received data will not be sensed at the right time, and will be incorrect. If the format is incorrect, if the receiver expects eight data bits, and the transmitter sends seven, the received word will be incorrect. This may or may not be caught by the parity bit.

Can the receiver derive clock information from the data stream, without prior knowledge of the baud rate? Yes, if special characters (sync words) are sent first. The format has to be agreed-upon. When the receiver sees a state transition on the line, it takes this to mean the leading edge of the start bit. It starts a local timer, and stops the timer, when the line state changes. This means the first data bit has to have the opposite state from a start bit. The receiver now knows the width of a bit, and divides this by two and start sampling the data bits in the middle..

If special characters are used, the receiver can guess the format of the data format to a good degree of accuracy. Given the initial guess, the receiver can transmit a request byte back to the original transmitter for a specific character, which then nails down the format. Note that this is not generally implemented in hardware UARTS, but can be accomplished in software.

In full duplex systems, data can be sent and received simultaneously over the link. This means the communications link has to have twice the capacity of a half-duplex link, which only allows the transmission of data in one direction at a time. Each link has a practical maximum rate of transmission, which is called the communication channel capacity. It is the upper bound to the amount of information that can be successfully transferred on the channel. That depends on noise, which corrupts the received information. Claude Shannon derived the concept of channel capacity, and provided an equation to calculate it. It is related to the signal to noise ratio of the channel.

In a Master/Slave system, one device is master and others are slaves. The master can initiate messages to individual slave units. This scheme is typically used in bus systems. The master can also broadcast a message to all units. In a Multi-Master scheme there is more than one master, and an arbitration scheme is necessary. This usually is implemented with a protocol for other devices than the current master to request bus mastership, which is then granted when feasible or convenient.

In a Peer-Peer scheme, on the other hand, there is no master, everyone is equal. This is the scheme used for Ethernet. If two units transmit at the same time, the transmission is garbled, and each unit retries after a random wait. If the randomness scheme works, this scheme is highly effective.

Baud rate generation is handled locally at a transmitter or receiver by a crystal oscillator. It is usually 16 times the bit rate, to provide adequate sampling of the incoming signal for receivers. It can be selected to several values. The sample clock can be different on the receiver and transmitter, but the baud rate must be the same.

Parity is a simple error control mechanism for communications and storage. We add an extra bit to the word, so we can adjust parity. Parity is based on the mathematical concept of even (evenly divisible by two) or odd. In binary, a number is even if its least-significant (rightmost) digit is zero (0).

For example, in ASCII,

A = 41$_{16}$ = 0100 0001 2 (1's) = even
B = 42$_{16}$ = 0100 0010 2 (1's) = even
C = 43$_{16}$ = 0100 0011 3 (1's) = odd

If we want to always have even parity, we would make the extra bit = 0 for A & B, 1 for C, etc.

If we want to get fancy, there are other schemes that use multiple bits to allow detection, and even correction, of multiple bit errors.

I/O on the chip

The 80x86 architecture has specific I/O instructions, and an I/O space separate from the memory space. The is different from architectures like the Motorola M68000, which have memory mapped I/O. This scheme will work on the Intel architecture as well.

The I/O space of the x86 family consists of a series of 8-bit locations, 64k of these for input, and 64k for output. Thus, a 16-bit I/O address is used. You might call these 8-bit locations "ports".

Let's talk about the ins and outs. We can input to or output from a register by specifying the port number, whether as a literal, or contained in the DX register.

Example:

        IN 10, AX   ; input from Port 10 to the AX register

        IN DX, AX   ; get input from the port specified in DX and put it in AX

        OUT BX, 10   ; output register BX contents to Port 10

        OUT BX,DX   : output register BX contents to port specified in DX

When we are running under an operating system, we will want to do our I/O with operating system calls, to let the opsys co-ordinate the I/O. If we have an embedded system, where we are the only program running, we can do direct I/O.

Memory

There are many types of memory used with the current cpu's. Most memory types are supported, if the word sizes and timing match. There is a small amount of memory on the CPU chip itself. This would be the various registers, and in later versions of the chip, cache memory. Most of the primary memory is placed on the same circuit board as the cpu, and can be soldered in place, or can take the form of plug-in modules. This memory is random-access. Non-volatile memory retains its contents without applied power. Some of it will be persistent, read-only memory, but more will be read-write, volatile memory. Secondary memory, with rotating magnetic disks, may be used along with optical disks for large offline storage. Flash memory, a type of persistent storage, is coming down in cost and up in capacity to be considered as an alternative to disks.

Computer memory is organized in a hierarchy. We would like to have large amounts of low power, fast, non-volatile storage. These requirements are mutually exclusive. The memory closest to the CPU is fast, random-access, volatile, and semiconductor-based, but expensive. Secondary storage, such as disk, is slower, cheaper, persistent, and cheaper on a cost-per-bit basis. Backup storage, offline optical or magnetic, is still cheaper per bit, but may have a longer access time.

Other characteristics of interest include memory latency, the time it takes to access the requested item, and throughput, the read or write rate of the memory device. Some memory may have a relatively slow latency, but a very high throughput, once things get going.

All-in-all, we have come a long way since computers stored bits as acoustic waves in a pool of mercury.

RAM

In RAM, random access memory, any element is accessible in the same clock time, as opposed to sequential media, such a tape or a disk. In sequential media, the access time varies, and depends on the order of access. This is true for disks, where the item requested probably just went by the read heads, and another rotation of the platter is required. Mechanical systems, in operation, tend to wear out due to mechanical causes. Electrical systems wear out as well, usually in a longer time.

A memory can be considered as a black-box with two functions, read and write. With the write function, we present the memory with two inputs: the data item, and an address. There is no output. The memory associates the data item with the address and remembers it. On the read function, we present the memory with the address, and expect to get back the data item previously associated with it.

Other design choices in memory include volatility. The memory may forget after a period of time. That's not good. Although, depending on the timing, the data can be read out and written back just in time.

Is there such a thing as totally non-volatile memory? One of the earliest memory types, magnetic core, was persistent when the power was turned off. It is unclear how long the data was retained. When compact disks, an optical media, first came out, the advertised lifetime was reported as 100 years. This has since been reduced, with some cd's and dvd's becoming unreadable in a period of several years. (A dvd is a cd with a greater capacity, because the wavelength of the laser light used is smaller, so the bits are closer together). If you want to see persistent color graphical information, the cave paintings at Lascaux in France are more than 17,000 years old, and still maintain their meaning. Magnetic hard disks do not forget their contents when the power is turned off. If they are properly stored, and not exposed to bumps, magnetic fields, and extremes of temperature, they seem to have the best data retention characteristics of currently available media. Exchangeable floppy disks have alignment problems in their readers, and magnetic tape drives use a fragile media that is susceptible to damage and environmental effects.

Volatile memory includes static semiconductor ram and dynamic ram. Static ram uses a flip-flop, and retains its contents as long as the power remains. Static ram is faster, less dense, and consumes more power than dynamic ram. Dynamic RAM is more dense, usually by a power of 4, due to a simpler structure, but requires refresh. It forgets in fractions of a second, because the information is stored as a charge on a capacitor, which leaks away. Why would anyone use this as a storage media? It is cheap, easily mass produced, the "forget" time is eons to a computer chip, and the overhead of the refresh operation is minimal. The CPU usually does the refresh, because the memory is not usable during that time. The memory can be organized into sections, so a refresh in one section still allows access in others. Some DRAM is self-refreshing. In the IBM-pc architecture, a fake-dma is used to signal a refresh operation in progress. .

Non-volatile memory includes various types of read-only memory, and battery-backed static ram which has a life of several years, depending on the battery source.

Even read-only memory is written at least at once. Actually, a ROM (read-only memory) can be manufactured with a specific pattern of 1's and 0's built in. For prototyping, various types of programmable read-only memory are used. These can be written and erased multiple times. Earlier, ultraviolet light was used to erase the devices to an all-1's state. These chips had glass windows. Later, the contents became reprogrammable or alterable with higher voltage levels, and could be modified in-circuit. Both the ultraviolet-erasable versions (UV-PROM's) and the Electrically alterable forms (EEPRoms) tended to forget over a period of years. Before this phenomenon was understood, these types of parts were included in shipped systems, that failed in later use. The IBM AT's BIOS was one example, and similar embedded systems were used for certain subway fare card machines.

The evolution of this is flash memory. Flash can be programmed in-circuit, and is random-access for read. To write flash, a block is erased to all "1", and selected bits are written to "0". The write operation is slower than the read. In addition, although the device can be read indefinitely, there is an upper limit to the number of times it can be written. This is on the order of a million times in current technology, but this can be accomplished in under a second with the wrong application. Flash memory does wear out.

Write-only memory is of no particular interest.

Memory organization and addressing

Semiconductor memory, like all current microelectronics, is a 2-dimensional structure. Thus, density usually goes up by a factor of four, as we double the width and the height. Memory is a very regular structure, amenable to mass production.

In random access memory we address bytes, or words. We get a collection of bits every time we read memory. To address individual bits within a word, we need to use the logical operations (AND, OR) to single out bits within a word.

Caches

A cache is a temporary memory buffer for data. It is placed between the processor and the main memory. The cache is smaller, but faster than the main memory. Being faster, it is more expensive, so it serves as a transition to the main store. They may be several levels of cache (L1, L2, L3), the one closest to the processor having the highest speed, commensurate to the processor. That closest to the main memory has a lower speed, but is still faster than the main memory. The cache has faster access times, and becomes valuable when items are accessed multiple times. Cache is transparent to the user; it has no specific address.

We may have different caches for instructions and data, or a unified cache for both. Code is usually accessed in linear fashion, but data items are not. In a running program, the code cache is never written, simplifying its design. The nature of accessing for instructions and data is different. On a read access, if the desired item is present in a cache, we get a cache hit, and the item is read. If the item is not in cache, we get a cache miss, and the item must be fetched from memory. There is a small additional time penalty in this process over going directly to memory (in the case of a miss). Cache works because, on the average, we will have the desired item in cache most of the time, by design.

Cache reduces the average access time for data, but will increase the worst-case time. The size and organization of the cache defines the performance for a given program. The proper size and organization is the subject of much analysis and simulation.

Caches introduce indeterminacy in execution time. With cache, memory access time is no longer deterministic. We can't tell, a priori, if an item is or is not in cache. This can be a problem in some real-time systems.

A working set is a set of memory locations used by a program in a certain time interval. This can refer to code or data. Ideally, the working set is in cache. The cache stores not only the data item, but a tag, which identifies where the item is from in main memory. Advanced systems can mark ranges of items in memory as non-cacheable, meaning they are only used once, and don't need to take up valuable cache space.

For best performance, we want to keep frequently-accessed locations in fast cache. Also, cache retrieves more than one word at a time, it retrieves a "line" of data, which can vary in size. Sequential accesses are faster after an initial access (both in cache and regular memory) because of the overhead of set-up times.

Writing data back to cache does not necessarily get it to main memory right away. With a write-through cache, we do immediately copy the written item to main memory. With a write-back cache, we write to main memory only when a location is removed from the cache.

Many locations can map onto the same cache block. Conflict misses are easy to generate: If array A uses locations 0, 1, 2, … and array b uses locations 1024, 1025, 1026, …, the operation a[i] + b[i] generates conflict misses in a cache of size 1024.

Caches, then, provide a level of performance increase at the cost of complexity due to temporal or spatial locality of the data. The program is not aware of the location of the data, whether it is in cache or main memory. The only indication is the run time of the program.

Cache hierarchy

This includes the L1, L2, L3 caches. L1 is the smallest cache, located closest to the cpu, usually on the same chip. Some cpu's have all three levels on chip. Each of the levels of cache is a different size and organization, and has different policies, to optimize performance at that point.

A key parameter of cache is the replacement policy. The replacement policy strategy is for choosing which cache entry to overwrite to make room for a new data. There are two popular strategies: random, and least-recently used (LRU). In random, we simply choose a location, write the data back to main memory, and refill the cache from the new desired location. In least recently used scenario, the hardware keeps track of cache accesses, and chooses the least recently used item to swap out.

As long as the hardware keeps track of access, it can keep track of writes to the cache line. If the line has not been written into, it is the same as the items in memory, and a write-back operation is not required. The flag that keeps track of whether the cache line has been written into is called the "dirty" bit. This book does discuss the dirty bits of computer architecture.

Note that we are talking about cache as implemented in random access memory of varying speeds. The concept is the same for memory swapped back and forth to rotating disk; what was called virtual memory in mainframes.

Cache organization

In a fully-associative cache, any memory location can be stored anywhere in the cache. This form is almost never implemented. In a direct-mapped cache, each memory location maps onto exactly one cache entry. In an N-way set-associative cache, each memory location can go into one of n sets. Direct mapped cache has the best hit times. Fully associative cache has the lowest miss rates.

TLB

The Translation Lookaside Buffer (TLB) is a cache used to expedite the translation of virtual to physical memory address. It holds pairs of virtual and translated (physical addresses). If the required translation is present (meaning it was done recently), the process is speeded up.

Caches have a direct effect on performance and determinacy, but the system designer does not always have a choice, when the caches are incorporated as part of the cpu. In this case, the system designer needs to review the cache design choices to ensure it is commensurate with the problem being address by the system.

Buffers

Buffers are data structures used to hold items temporarily. We assume data is arriving (or departing) continuously, and any given item has a finite lifetime. Buffers are used when there is a difference between the rate when data arrives or leaves, and the rate at which it can be processed. A circular buffer allows overwrites. Indices or pointers are used to address data in the buffer, and need to be continuously updated. Buffers are implemented in memory. They can be user-defined, or included in the hardware.

Queue

A queue is a first-in, first-out data structure in memory that is a sort of elastic buffer. It is useful for data that arrives or departs on an irregular basis, not necessarily in a smooth stream. The output of the queue can be accessed on a regular basis, as long as the size of the queue is such that data can be held without an overflow. Queues are defined in memory, and are managed with pointers. They can be hardware or software entities.

Memory Management

Virtual memory is an abstraction. We pretend we have more memory than is available in the system, but we only see a portion of this memory at a given time. The contents of the physical memory that we do have are managed by hardware, and are swapped in and out from secondary storage. Data is transferred in blocks. The program can be written without worrying about how much memory is available. Actually, if we add more physical memory, the systems will run faster, because fewer swaps are required.

Memory management allows a program to run anywhere in memory without being recompiled. It provides a level of protection and isolation between programs to prevent overwriting. It removes restrictions on the size of available memory by the virtual memory technique.

A memory management unit (MMU) translates memory addresses from logical/virtual to physical. This adds the overhead of translation to each memory access. In addition, the access time for the secondary storage may be a million times slower than for the primary memory, but it will have 100's of times large capacity, and certainly be cheaper. There is also the energy consumption issue.

When the CPU accesses a desired item, it may be present in the memory, or not. If not, the process generates a Page fault, resulting in an interrupt, with a request for data item not currently resident. This requires clever programming to be an efficient process. Too many misses, and the process bogs down in overhead.

The scheme requires data structures to keep track of what range of data addresses is actually present in memory, and registers or tables to allow arbitrary mappings of logical to physical addresses.

There are two basic schemes: segmented and paged. Paged usually deals with fixed sized blocks of memory, and segmentation is more flexible in terms of size. Segmentation and paging can be combined as in the x86 architecture.

The address translation process was handled by a separate MMU chip, although this function is now incorporated into the CPU. The operating system is in charge of the data structures and the details of virtual memory management.

Memory management in the x86/pc was very rudimentary before the introduction of Protected Mode with the Intel 80286 architecture.

Software Elements of a Computer

Program (definition):
A magic spell cast over a computer allowing it to
translate input statements into error messages.

You don't learn much about the underlying structure of the hardware by programming in a higher order language such as c or Java.

Instruction Set Architecture (ISA) of the 80x86 Family

The ISA of the 80x86 family is defined by Intel Corporation. Besides Intel, numerous other manufacturers make or have made 80x86 family members and derivatives. These include AMD, Cyrix, NEC, and others. Specialized embedded versions of the 80x86 ISA evolved. The instruction set has been emulated in software on competing processors, such as the IBM/Motorola/Apple PowerPC. The instruction set can be emulated in hardware in chips such as the IMS 3250, or the PowerPC 615.

The original ISA is a 16-bit architecture, extended to 32-bits with the Pentium series of processors. The next generation of chips are a 64-bit architecture, the extension to ISA-64, which maintains compatibility with ISA-32.

Programmers model of the x86

The Programmer's view of the x86 Instruction Set Architecture (ISA) includes:

The memory model, the registers (data), and the instructions (operations on data).

The Intel 8086 was a 16-bit processor, circa 1978. It was designed as a follow-on to the earlier successful 8-bit 8080 processor. There were big advantages in going to a 16-bit word, and the associated 8087 co-processor provided floating point capability. Software comparability was not maintained.

76

The 8086 provided fourteen 16-bit registers. Four of these were general purpose, and there were four pointer/index, four segment, a flags register, and the program counter. With 16 address bits, the processor could addresses 1 megabyte of memory. There were 135 basic instructions, including multiply and divide, and many variations. The chip provided support for the BCD data format, and had a separate I/O space with 65,000 input and 65,000 output ports. The I/O ports were 8-bits in size.

Status flags are automatically set by ALU operations, and can be read by the program. These allow for the implementation of data dependent branches, like "branch on zero." The status flags include:

- Carry flag, CF, set on high order bit carry or borrow.
- Parity flag PF, set if even.
- Aux. Carry - key to BCD operations, set on carry or borrow from lower 4 bits to upper 4 bits.
- Zero flag – ZF, set if results were zero.
- Trap flag - if set, interrupt occurs after each instruction.
- Interrupt enable (programmer settable) - if not set, cpu ignores interrupts
- Direction flag - set by instruction, controls direction of string moves, high to low, or low to big.
- Overflow flag - set if signed result cannot be represented

Assembly Language

"Nobody should be allowed to program in assembly language" Jim Isaak, Computer Design, Jan. 1, 1987

"When in doubt, try brute force." anonymous, attributed to Attila, et al.

The assembly language of a processor, expressed in the ISA definition, defines the data types and the operations the processor can handle. We study the ISA so we can gain an understanding of the underlying architecture. The x86 ISA is a good, but complicated example.

An Assembler is a program that takes textual input, and produces binary code and storage allocations for a processor.

Assembly language syntax includes data structures, instructions, and directives. The data structures include the data formats, integers, packed and unpacked bcd, bytes, double words, floating point, that the processor can handle. This defines the format of storage for instructions and data. The instructions defines the logical, mathematical, and flow-of-control operations that can be performed on the data. Directives are in-line directives to the assembler program, and do not generate code or require storage.

At times, a programmer may need to delve into assembly language. You may need to write a device driver. As opposed to general languages such as c or Java, the assembly language is unique to the hardware architecture. The concepts are generally the same across assemblers for different architectures. A statement in assembly usually maps directly to a single machine language instruction, where a statement in a higher order language would result in multiple machine language instructions. A knowledge of assembly language, even if you never use it, gives you a better insight into the internal operations of the computer. Each assembly language, for each different processor, is different.

The assembly process starts with an editor to create the source file; the assembler program to create the object file; a linker/loader program to create an executable module, and perhaps a debugger program, that runs alongside your code, in a simulated environment. The debugger takes up time and space, which is important to remember, but provides needed visibility into the running program.

If you follow the right conventions, your assembly module can be linked with Higher order languages such as Pascal, C/C++, JAVA, and others. Each HOL will have its own conventions on how it interacts with assembly language on a particular processor.

Assembly language programs are created by a text editor. It is highly recommended that they be extensively documented at creation. This will help the author understand what he or she meant later. Assembly language is full of details, and these can get easily lost over time. There is probably no such thing as too much documentation.

An assembler is a program that produces binary code from symbolic representations. There is generally a one:one relationship between the input statements and the output, and the operations and data items map directing to functional units and registers.

The assembler program usually works in two passes through the source code. On the first pass, the symbol table is built. On the second pass, the binary instructions are generated. The assembler's job is easier than the compiler's, because most of the translation of instructions from source to binary (machine-readable) format is very simple. Pre-assembled libraries can be included with the source code, and the binary output from the assembler can be linked with binary output form a compiler or compilers.

The linking process involves translating the relative addresses from the assembly or compilation process to absolute addresses in the target memory. At assembly time, some label values might not yet be defined. This is true for references to external labels. The linker's job is to resolve all memory addresses to those that exist in the target memory. Note that this allows the program to be moved (relocated) in memory at this step, without changing the source code. The output of the linker is the binary code to be loaded into memory, at specific addresses. Dynamic linking allows for sharing of common modules.

A device driver is a special piece of software that interfaces the system to an external device. It is specifically associated with the device, and its details. These are good candidates for assembly language programming. Writing a device drive is something of a rite of passage, and requires intimate knowledge of the hardware.

The compilation process

The step that translates your algorithm from an instantiation in a higher order language such as c into a language that the hardware understands is called compilation. Compilation involves both translation and optimization. Compilation can be done by hand, but it is certainly much easier with machine resources. It involves the translation of an algorithm or process, expressed in a user-friendly language, into a machine-readable format. It allows us to capture requirements and implement them in the unique hardware of the machine.

The compiler, itself a program, takes our code as input, and produces error messages – actually, it produces code for the target machine, usually in the form of assembly language. The higher order language statements, somewhat algebraic in form, translate into multiple assembly language statements. The compilation stage is followed by an assembly stage. Assembly language usually translates 1:1 into machine language.

The program is not necessarily compiled into one big lump of code – it may be modular. This allows code reuse. Modules may be stored in a library, and attached to the main program as required. Think of a square root routine as an example. The program that takes the output of the compiler, the various programs from the code library, and possibly some assembly language and puts it all together into one module is the linker.

The quality of the produced code reflects on the use of cpu resources, memory usage, performance (throughput), and quality.

The compiler can also do optimizations, both machine-independent, and machine or architecture dependent. We first have to understand what type of optimization (if any) is required: for space or time. We might require a small program, a fast program, or a small, fast program. In the embedded computer world, we may optimize for energy use, or power consumption. Optimization is also processor-specific. We are working with the IA-32 architecture, but it is implemented in different ways by different chip makers. What might be optimal for one approach may be exactly the wrong thing to do for another. Without instruction dependencies, the Pentium should be twice as fast as a '386. Because of dependencies, the theoretical number is 1.7 times as fast. In actuality, it is more like 1.2. This is because not every pair of instructions is independent. Many instructions rely on the results from the previous. The x86 architecture is difficult to optimize for. There are not enough registers, and the variable length instructions are difficult to pipeline.

Although the Pentium has two of the '386's integer engines, they are not identical. Only one has the barrel shifter. Shift operations have to be steered to that unit, or the flow of instructions will slow down. This can be done by code re-ordering by the compiler, or at runtime.

We need to ensure that our intent is not optimized out of the program. Static or machine-independent optimization techniques include dead-code optimization, where the compiler optimizer decides a piece of code that seems to do nothing useful. The compiler can also get rid of loop overhead, and put multiple copies of code inline. This approach trades space for time. The resultant code is more optimized for a pipeline architecture. It is sometimes possible to combine two loops into one, eliminating some loop overhear. Loop tiling involves breaking one loop into a nest of loops for the facilitation of memory accesses. In these cases, the compiler must have intimate details of the pipeline architecture.

If the underlying architecture does not use a pipelined architecture, then an instruction order that satisfies the data dependencies is fine. However, it is reasonable to assume that modern architectures are pipelined. A pipeline is a set of processing elements in series. The output of one is the input to the next. This allows overlapping execution of multiple instructions. In the classical fetch-execute model, the first stage does the fetch-ings, and the second stage does the executing (which might involve operand fetches). Pipelines are analogous to production lines.

Once a pipeline is full, an instruction can complete in each clock cycle. There is a latency in getting the pipeline filled, and in refilling it.

Operating system: what it is; what it does

An operating system (OS) is a software program that manages computer hardware resources, and provides common services for execution of various application software. Without an operating system, a user cannot run an application program on their computer, unless the application program is self-booting.

For hardware functions such as input and output and memory allocation, the operating system acts as an intermediary between application programs and the computer hardware, although the application code is usually executed directly by the hardware and will frequently call the OS or be interrupted by it. Operating systems are found on almost any device that contains a computer. The OS functions are done by software, whether we call that software an OS or not.

An operating system manages computer resources, including
- o   Memory.
- o   I/O.
- o   Interrupts.
- o   Tasks/processes/Threads of execution.

The operating system arbitrates and enforces priorities

The early operating systems for the x86 architecture included versions of DOS (disk operating systems) from Microsoft Corporation, Digital Research, and IBM. To take advantage of the memory mapping and protection mechanisms, these simple DOS's evolved into Microsoft Windows, Digital Research's Concurrent CPM, and IBM's OS/2. With 32-bit processors, variations of Unix began to appear. Microsoft Windows is now the dominant player, with linux and bsd (Unix variations) in use, and hundreds of niche efforts as well.

It is useful to look at DOS, because it is the basis for the Windows operating system. Some of the features persist through many hardware generations. On the IBM pc architecture, the operating system consisted of two parts, the BIOS in read-only memory, and the DOS, stored on disk, initially, insertable floppy disks, and later, a hard disk. Other storage media used on the early machines included magnetic tape. The DOS was brought in to memory by the bootloader on the BIOS. Not all the DOS was brought in at once; that wouldn't have left any space for user programs. The resident portion determined what services the user was requesting, and read additional transient portions of the operating system as needed.

The BIOS concept was to decouple the DOS code functions from the hardware details. It represents a hardware abstraction layer. The concept goes back to Gary Kildall's CP/M program (Control Program for Microprocessors, for 8-bit cpu's), but he borrowed the concepts from Digital Equipment Corp. The rest of the operating system, whether it be DOS, Windows, Unix, or whatever, relies on the BIOS. Thus, the BIOS has provided a consistent interface to additional functionality – a layered approach. The BIOS concept persists, but the implementation is nearing the end of life as systems require a faster boot time, and more functionality.

The DOS (using this in a generic sense) can then be then hardware independent. The BIOS is hardware dependent, and initially written in assembly language. Besides desktop and server operating systems, specialized operating systems for embedded systems applications can be used.

The BIOS functions include set-up after power-on reset, including hardware checking and setup. The BIOS provides rudimentary I/O services for a limited range of devices such as the keyboard, screen, and disks. The BIOS also provides a boot function, whose job it is to go to side 0, track 0, sector 1 of the default boot device, and read what is there into memory, and then jump to that routine. That hopefully would be the system boot record.

The disk resident services that the DOS provides are more complex. The system boot record contains enough smarts to load the system files. The DOS defines a file structure on the disk, handles user input and other I/O, and provides a series of commands and services for the user. The DOS relies on a series of information collected by the BIOS on system configuration. Because not all of the DOS program is resident, the available commands are handled by intrinsic routines, if simple, and by loadable modules if they are more complex. For example, a disk directory can be done with the intrinsic code, but a file copy will required additional modules to be loaded. One concept of importance is the Batch file. This is a file of system commands that can be executed. An important batch file is AUTOEXEC.COM, which is executed automatically after the boot process, the do any additional system configuration required. The DOS also loads system-specific device drivers (I/O handlers). Before this, device drivers had to be assembled into the operating system.

The DOS file structure is built upon linked lists. The directory file contains lists of files and information about them. It uses a 32-byte entry per file, containing the file name, extension, attributes, date and time, and the starting location of the file on disk.

The File Allocation Table (FAT) is a built map of allocated clusters on the disk. A cluster is the default unit of storage. It's size is a trade-off between efficiency of storage, and efficiency of access. A size of 256 bytes to 1024 bytes worked well in the early days. Two copies of the FAT are kept by the system, and these are on fixed locations of the storage media.

A directory file has entries for all of the files on the disk. The name of the file is in 8.3 format, meaning an 8 character file name, and a 3-character extension. The extension tells the type of the file, executable program, word processing, etc. By DOS convention, when a file is erased, the first character of the name is changed to the character $E5_{16}$. The data is not lost at this point. If nothing else happens in the mean-time, the file can be un-erased, and recovered. However, the E5 signifies the space the file occupied is now available for use.

Various file attribute bits are kept. The file can be marked as read-only, hidden, reserved system type, and bits indicate a directory field, a volume label (name of a storage volume, like, "disk1"), and whether the file has been archived (saved). There is a 16-bit date code in the format (year-1980)*512 + month * 32 + day. (thought exercise – when do we have a problem?). The starting cluster number in a directory is kept as a word value. This limits us to 2^{16} clusters.

The FAT was originally 12-bits, but later extended to 16. Eventually, this was extended to 32-bits for Windows, and is no longer DOS compatible. Entries in the FAT map the clusters on the storage media. These indicate used, available, bad, and reserved clusters.

The user communicates with the operating system (BIOS/DOS) with service requests via interrupts. BISO services include handlers for I/O to the first two serial (comm) ports, for the first two printer (parallel) ports, several simple video modes, some rudimentary disk I/O (NOT file I/O), and accessing the equipment list. Interrupts less than 20_{16} are used to communicate with the BIOS, but the Intel-defined hardware interrupts in this range are untouched.

Disk services are requested from the BIOS by a user program using Interrupt 13_{16}. These include functions such as reset, diagnose, seek to a cylinder, read, write, verify after write, and format. As the disk head moves radially, it defines a series of changing cylinders across all of the platters of the disk. On a single disk surface, we divide the circular track into sectors or segments. Each platter has a read/write head associated with it, sometimes, two, if the platter can be used on both the top and bottom surfaces.

Here is an example of a read disk request for service from a user program to the BIOS. First, we define a buffer to hold the data, and place the address of the buffer in the ES:BX pair. Then we put the drive number in DL. The head number goes in DH, the sector number in CL, the track number in CH, and the number of sectors to read in AL. We put 02 in AH, and interrupt interrupt 13. Seems hard, right? Yes, because we are below the level of the defined file structure. There are a lot of hardware details we are not really interested in. Some program (the DOS) needs to hide these details from us, handle them transparently, and let us live in the dream world of files. Files are an abstraction. Disks have heads, cylinders, sectors, and such.

The BIOS can tell us if the disk we are access is a permanent one (hard disk) or uses replaceable media (floppies). If using floppies, it can tell us if the media has been changed since the last access.

For serial I/O services, the BIOS can write an ASCII character, or read one. Initially, the IBM pc had an audio cassette unit for offline storage. Bits were saved as audio tones on tape. This was not a fast media. Later, these services in the BIOS were redefined to handle power management services. The BIOS allows us the read the game joysticks, which have several switches, and four analog inputs. We can also request or set the system time, which is maintained by a small battery-powered clock chip. The original set of video services included support of a light pen, but this rapidly became obsolete when the mouse came along. The original IBM pc contained the BASIC language in a ROM on the system board. This was patented, and no other manufacturer could implement this feature.

The BIOS provides the memory size with an Interrupt 12 request. Interrupt 11 returns the equipment list in register AX. This tells us the number of disk drives, whether a math coprocessor is present, the video mode, the number of serial ports, and the number of printers in the system.

DOS services are invoked with a single interrupt, 21_h, with the service request in the AH register. DOS services were extended to support new hardware configurations, including the mouse, the network card, CD-ROM, power management functions, and memory management. As the DOS is file-oriented, we can request reading a specific file name, and DOS looks this up in the FAT and fetches the file for us. The FAT itself is a file, but a memory resident copy can be kept to speed operations.

DOS file services include creation and deletion of files and directories, opening and closing a file, read and write, rename, and change or set the attributes. Recall that a directory is simply a file that contains the names and locations of other files.

Interrupt 19_{16} is used to reboot the system. It reads the data at cylinder 0, sector 1 of the default boot device into memory location 0000:7C00, and then jumps to that location. For better or for worse.

The Intel x86 instruction set

This section will discuss the storage elements on the cpu chip (the registers), the logical and arithmetic operations on data, and the ways to change the flow of control in the program. The principals are the same for any digital computer, but the implementation varies.

The registers

First, we need to introduce the registers, which are temporary working memory on the cpu chip itself. They hold data items temporarily, and can serve as inputs to, and the output from the arithmetic logic unit. Some registers are involved in addressing memory. The cpu has other registers that are not visible to the programmer.

The default register size is 16 bits. The general purpose registers are named AX, BX, CX, and DX. Each 16-bit register is actually two adjacent 8-bit registers.

        AX = AH, AL
        BX = BH, BL
        CX = CH, CL
        DX = DH, DL

The 16-bit registers were extended to 32 bits. These general purpose registers are called EAX, EBX, ECX, EDX. (extended AX, etc.). The AX register is the lower 16 bits of the 32-bit EAX register, just as the AL register is the lower 8 bits of the 16 bit AX.

The 16-bit pointer/index registers are: SP, BP, SI, DI. These are the stack pointer, the base pointer, the source index, and the destination index registers. Pointer/index registers hold addresses.

The extended 32-bit pointer index registers are ESP, EBP, ESI, EDI. Extended stack pointer, etc.

87

The 16-bit segment registers are CS, DS, ES, SS. These are for the Code segment, the Data segment, the extra (data) segment, and the stack segment. Segment registers hold part of the address.

The 80386 and subsequent architectures have two additional "data" type segment registers, FS and GS.

Instruction syntax

Some instructions will only have a source; some will only have a destination; some will have both; a few have neither. For example, the stack instructions have implied operands. Mostly, in the x86 word, the destination is specified first, then the source. Thus we operate from right to left.

Example:

    MOV destination, source

This convention of ordering is defined by the assembler. The other option is possible.

    MOV source, destination

    Make sure you know the convention of your assembler before proceeding.

The Move operation requires two operands. These are the source parameter (what to move) and the destination (where to move to). The move is actually a COPY, because the source remain unchanged.

The MOV instruction is used to transfer a byte, word (double-byte), or doubleword (quad-byte) from one storage location to another. Both operands must be the same size, and no flags are affected.

What are these flags? Flags are binary indicators that are set automatically by the hardware, and can be checked in software. They allow for data-dependent changes in the flow of control. Typical flags include Negative, Overflow, Parity, Zero.

When we move data from memory to the processor, that is sometimes called a Load operation. When we move data from the processor to memory, that is sometimes referred to as a Store operation. In the IA-86 architecture, we can move data between processor registers, but not between memory locations directly. That operation takes a load operation followed by a store.

The MOV Instruction syntax is fairly simple:

MOV destination, source
MOV {register or memory},{register or memory or immediate value}

We can move an Immediate to a Segment register, but it takes two steps. We need to move the immediate item to a general purpose register, and then move the general purpose register to the segment register. The direct path does not exist on the cpu chip.

MOV AX, DVAL   ;move value DVAL to AX register
MOV DS, AX   ;move AX register to DS register

To do a memory to memory move, we have to do a load followed by a store, involving a general purpose register.

MOV AX, MEM1   ;move the contents of MEM1 to AX register (load)
MOV MEM2, AX   ;move AX register to MEM2 (store)

Similarly when we want to move a segment register contents to another segment register, we need to go through an intermediate general purpose register.

MOV AX, DS   ;temporarily, move DS to AX
MOV ES, AX   ;now move AX to ES

We can exchange data between two locations (swap) in one step with an exclusive or (XOR) operation, called Exchange.

XCHG <register or memory>, <register or memory>

For a simplified table look-up, we can use the translate (XLAT) instruction. This converts a given 8-bit pattern to another 8-bit pattern. We first need to set up the translate table in memory It has 256 entries. The start address of table should be in the register BX. The input data should be in the register AL, which is used as the table index. When we execute the XLAT instruction, it fetches the value at the location in the table pointed to by AL.

AL = output value = Table {input}

We can transfer flags to and from the internal flags register (set by the hardware)to general purpose registers. The LAHF instruction puts the lower 8 bits of the flags register into the AH register. The SAHF instruction puts the contents of the AH register into the lower 8 bits of the flags register. The flags SF, ZF, AF, PF, CD go to bits 7,6,4,2,0.

Data size conversion

In the 80x86 architecture, there is no moving of data between registers of different sizes allowed. To go from a smaller to a larger register, we have to consider whether the value is considered signed or unsigned. In the two cases, the most significant bit means something different, and the meaning (if not the bit) needs to be preserved. To go from a larger to a smaller word size, something has to get discarded.

Conversions of signed values

The instructions to convert the word sizes of signed entities include:

CBW - convert byte to word, 8-bit AL to 16- bit AX
CWD - convert word to doubleword, 16-bit AX to 32-bit DX:AX
CWDE - convert word to doubleword, 16-bit AX to 32-bit in EAX
CDQ - convert doubleword to quadword, 32-bit in EAX to 64-bit in EDX:EAX

Note that specific input and output registers are specified. When a smaller to a larger conversion is done on a signed entity, the sign is extended into the upper part of the word. We would place a smaller entity into a larger register to gains some "headroom" for further calculations. In some cases, a register pair is required.

Unsigned

For conversion of a smaller to a larger register representation, we need to manually set the upper register (or part of the register) to zero. For example, an 8-bit entity in register AL can be converted to an equivalent 16-bit entity in AX, if we makes sure the upper part of AX (i.e., AH), is set to zero. How to force registers to zero will be explained in the section on logical operations.

Loading pointers

Pointer values are addresses; they point to something of interest. Thus, they have a size commensurate with the addressing of the memory. When we want to get the address of an item, not its contents or value, we need to load the address. There is an instruction for that.

The Concept of Distance

We need to know the distance between where we are, and where we are referring. The distance is measured in address bytes.

Different lengths

"Near" means in same segment, and requires a 16-bit offset, because a segment is 64k bytes, addressed by a 16-bit value. "Far" means anywhere in the address space, and requires 32 bits, that is, a new 16-bit segment register contents, and a 16-bit offset.

LEA, Load Effective Address is used to calculate the effective address of an operand, which may not be known until run time. There may be run-time calculations that prevent the value from being known at compile time.

These two instructions are the same, for direct address:

```
        LEA    DX, VAR
        MOV    DX, OFFSET VAR     ;Here we use the word "Offset" to
signal the
                                  ; assembler we want the address of
the item,
                                  ; not the value.
```

For indirect address, which is not known until we actually run the program, we do a:

```
        LEA    DX,VAR[SI]         ;value in [SI] not yet known
        OFFSET operator
```

If the address can be resolved at assembly time, this "OFFSET" operator returns the offset address of the expression:

```
        MOV  BX, OFFSET ARRAY        ; load the address of ARRAY
        into BX
```

Far pointers (32-bits in size) require 32-bit registers, or a pair of 16-bit registers.

```
        LEA, for far pointers (32-bits).
        LDS    DS:DI
        LES    ES:SI
        LFS, LGS similar
```

Defining data structures.

In assembly, we define our data structures to the assembler. These will contain the data to be operated upon by the program. These are done with assembler directives. Defining the data structures is a very important part of the programming process, and the definition of variables' characteristics has a major impact on program correctness, size, and run time.

Assembler directives

```
        DB     define bytes, 0 to 256 unsigned, -128 to 127 +signed
```

DW   define words, 0 to 64k unsigned, -32,768 to +32767

DD   define doublewords, 0 to 4 x 10^9, - 2 billion to + 2 billion +/- a little

We will do most of our work with integers, where the resolution = 1.

We can also define arrays of data, that can be predefined with a desired content.

Array DB	10 DUP (1)	; define a 10-element array of 1's
Array1 DW	100 DUP (87)	; define a 100-element array of 87's
Array2 DD	32 DUP (99999)	; define a 32 element array of 99999
Array3 DB	10 DUP (10 DUP ("A"))	; define a 100 (10x10) element array of "A"s
Buffer DB	256 DUP (?)	; define a buffer of size 256 bytes, uninitialized

Regardless of our fancy organizational concepts of our data, it will be stored in sequential memory address in memory. We may need to force alignment of data on word or doubleword boundaries for speed-of-access reasons. The program will be logically correct but slow if the data is not placed in memory correctly. A compiler can help with this. In assembly, you are on your own.

Stack Protocols

This section discusses how to use the stack data structure. The Stack Pointer(SP) contains the address of the current location of the top of the stack, relative to the Stack Segment register. The stack segment register puts the stack into a specific 64k segment. The stack pointer is the address within that segment.

The Base Pointer (BP) register is also relative to the stack segment, and can be used to point to a stack frame. A stack frame is a data structure you define in the stack. You need to know the definition of the order of the elements, and top address.

Protocol says that you PUSH data onto the stack and POP data off; PUSH and POP operations are used in pairs. We always want to have the same number of PUSHes (put-em-on) as POPs (take-em-off). Otherwise, we may make a mess in memory.

The stack is a zero, or implied address, operand. The operation happens at the top of the stack, where the stack pointer points.

syntax:
>PUSH <thing>
>POP   <thing>

where <thing> := register or memory. Where does it go? To the memory location at the top of the stack, which is a data structure defined in the stack segment, and pointed to by the stack pointer.

On 80186, '286, '386, and subsequent, we can do a PUSH Immediate Value.

The PUSH operation stores a two-byte operand on the stack and the stack pointer is then decremented by two; SP=SP-2. The stack grows downward (toward lower addresses) in memory. This is important to remember if code, data, and stack are in the same segment. The stack can extend down to bump into code of data extending up in memory. This can have some amusing consequences if the expanding stack overwrites the code.

The POP operation retrieves a two byte operand from the stack, and the stack pointer is incremented; SP=SP+2. The SP register is a byte counter, but it always points to a word (16-bit) boundary. Thus, it always changes by two. The CPU hardware takes responsibility of incrementing or decrementing the SP.

To reiterate, the data movement direction is, a PUSH decrements the SP, the stack expands, data moves toward lower addresses; a POP increments the SP, the stack shrinks toward upper memory.

94

OK, here's a stack question: Can you push the SP? Why, yes. You can push the SP, just like any other register. This pushes the contents of SP before the PUSH operation except, on the 8088/8086; here it pushes the contents of the SP after the PUSH.

The PUSHA, or push all, does all of the 16-bit general registers in order: AX, CX, DX, BX, SP, BP, SI, DI. The PUSHAD pushes all of the 32-bit general registers: EAX, ECX, EDX, EBX, ESP, EBP, ESI, EDI. Similarly, POPA pops all of the 16-bit general registers, and POPAD pops all of the 32-bit general registers.

We can push or pop the flags register with PUSHF and POPF. In the advanced architectures, we can push or pop the extended flags registers with PUSHFD and POPFD.

Putting register data on the stack for use later:

```
PUSH AX     ; to (SP); where SP points
PUSH BX     ; bx at (SP-2)
PUSH CX     ; cx at (SP-4)
```

Now, call a subroutine, which will automatically push the return address on the stack at location SP-6.

Within the subroutine, we can access the data thus:

```
MOV  AX, [SP+6]
MOV  BX, [SP+4]
MOV  CX, [SP+2]
SUB  SP, 6              ; this cleans up the stack pointer, restores its
```
correct value.

The stack is useful in storing transient information, and for passing information back and forth to subroutines without using dedicated memory locations.

Basic Math Operations

The first math operations we will consider are ADD, SUB, ADC (ADD, with carry in), and INC (Increment by 1).

The ADD operation adds two operands that are 8, 16 or 32 bit data; but both must be the same size. The operands may be in registers or memory. The operation automatically sets flags in the status register. INC is an unsigned operation; the carry flag is not updated.

The source is added to the destination, and the result is stored in the destination location. Thus, the previous value in the destination is overwritten.

When an addition generates a result too large for signed numbers, the **overflow** flag is set. When an addition generates a result too large for unsigned numbers, the **carry** flag is set. The hardware does not know if what we are adding is considered by us as signed or unsigned. It just does the math. The interpretation is left to us.

ADD timing (for immediate to accumulator mode) in machine cycles:

       8086   4 cycles
       80286 3 cycles
       80386 2 cycles
       80486 1 cycle

The interesting thing to note here is that processor architectures were improved to the goal of one-cycle instructions, over four generations of the hardware. At the same time, the processor clock, which controls the cycle time, also speeded up tremendously.

ADC is like ADD, with a carry in. It adds the two operands, plus the state of the carry bit before the instruction is executed. This is used for multi-word math; chained operations to add arbitrary length integers.

We can add arbitrary length integers, 16 bits at a time, by using a loop. We would use the CLC (clear carry) before entry to the loop the first time. The loop keeps track of the number of 16-bit parts (partial sums) we have completed.

INC is a single operand instruction; it adds one to the item of interest. It is a good time to point out the redundancy in the instruction set. INC is the same as adding "1". In most cases, there are several ways to accomplish the same thing. Some will be faster, some will be smaller, if that is a consideration.

SUB is used for subtraction. SBB is a SUB with borrow in. DEC means to subtract 1. NEG means to change sign. CMP is used to compare two items. It is just a subtract, but the results are not stored. The important thing is, the flags are set. If the two values are equal, the result is zero, and the ZERO flag will be set. This can be used by subsequent conditional branch instructions.

The SUB instruction works on 8, 16 or 32 bit data but both must be the same size
It can access registers or memory. It sets flags in status register. DEC is and unsigned operation, the carry flag not updated.

When a subtraction generates a result too small for signed numbers, the **carry** flag is set. (hint: carry = borrow, in 2's comp). When a subtraction generates a result too large for unsigned numbers, the **sign** flag is set. Again, the CPU doesn't know what we consider the data items to be, signed or unsigned.

8-BIT SUBTRACTION Example

```
        .DATA
MEM8 DB    122    ; arbitrary value
        .CODE
```

	SIGNED	UNSIGNED
MOV AL, 95	95	95
DEC AL	-1	-1
SUB AL, 23	-23	-23
	71	71
SUB AL, MEM8	-122	-122
	-51	205 & SIGN
MOV AH, 119	119	

SBB is SUB, with a borrow in. The operation subtracts the two operands, minus the state of the carry bit before the instruction is executed. As with ADC, this can be used for multi-word math; chained operations to subtract arbitrary length integers. We would use a loop, and use CLC (clear carry) before entry to the loop the first time.

The Decrement instruction takes a single operand, and subtracts 1.

Negate also takes a single operand. It is only used on signed numbers. It produces the proper two's complement value. It does this by subtracting the operand from zero, and setting the flags appropriately.

Logical operations

Recall that the logical operations on data are done on a bit-by-bit basis. These include NOT, AND, OR, XOR (exclusive OR), and TEST. Except for the NOT or negate operation, all the functions take two inputs.

The AND operation is a bit by bit operation on two sources where the output is 1 if and only if both inputs are 1. Otherwise the output is 0. We can use AND to clear specific bits. We would use a mask word, where the mask bit = 0 for bits to be cleared, and the mask bit = 1 for bits that are to stay unchanged.

Example:

```
MOV  AX, 00110101
AND  AX, 11111011        ; clear bit 2
```

One use for this would be to convert ASCII lower case to upper case; bit 5 should is clear in uppercase ASCII:

```
        AND   AL, 11011111b        ; ASCII value in AL will now be in
lower case.
```

The OR function is a logical (inclusive) or. The output is 1 if either input, or both inputs are 1. Otherwise the output is 0. We can use OR to set specific bits in a word. We would use a mask word, where the mask bit = 1 for bit positions to be set; and zero otherwise.

For example:

```
MOV  AX, 00110101b
OR   AX, 00001000b        ; force bit 3 of AX on (=1)
```

Another use for this operation is to OR an operand with itself, to set the zero flag.

```
         OR    BX,BX      ; is BX positive or negative?
         JG    POSITIVE
         JL    NEGATIVE
ZERO:
```

This is the same function as the compare, but the instruction is faster and smaller.

The XOR is an exclusive OR operation, meaning the output is 1 if either input is 1, but not both. Otherwise the output is zero. We can use XOR to toggle specific bits We would set up a mask word where the corresponding mask bit = 1 for toggle, =0 for unchanged.

Example:

```
MOV  AX, 00110101
XOR  AX, 00001000        ; toggle bit 3
```

We can also use XOR to clear a register. An XOR of an item with itself forces it to zero. This is an alternative to subtracting an item from itself, or MOVing a zero in to it. Different timings, different sizes, same result.

Example – these all do the same thing.

```
XOR  CX, CX        ;2 BYTES, 3 CLOCKS
```

```
MOV  CX, O          ;3 BYTES, 4 CLOCKS
SUB   CX, CX         ;2 BYTES, 3 CLOCKS
```

note: MOV doesn't affect flags, the other operations do.

The NOT operation takes a single operand and reverses the logical sense of the operand, bit by bit. It is a logical 1's complement.

We can do scanning for set bits on the 80386 and subsequent. The instructions are:

BSF - bit scan forward DATA
BSR - bit scan reverse DATA

These look for the first (or last) bit set in the data item. These work on 16- or 32-bit registers. The destination register contains the bit position; with the zero flag set.

The Bit Test (BT op1, op2) copies a single bit from operand1 to the carry flag (CF) which can then be tested. If operand2 is an immediate operand, it specifies the bit to be copied.

Bit Test and Complement (BTC) is like bit test, but the bit is complemented in the word, after copy to the CF.

Bit Test and Set (BTS) works like BTC, but the bit is set after the copy to CF.

BCD Operations

BCD numbers require four bits, and can be found in two variations, packed and unpacked, within an 8-bit byte. Unpacked has a single BCD digit in the lower 4 bits of the 8 bit byte, and in packed mode, two 4-bit bcd digits are in each byte. This effects how carry's between bcd digits are handled when we do math.

We can do the four standard math operations on either format of BCD digits: Add, Subtract, Multiply, and Divide.

The following names are standard, but unfortunate: single BCD digit per byte is called unpacked or ASCII, and two BCD digits per byte is called packed or Decimal format.

Unpacked BCD

Unpacked format has one BCD per byte, and is called "ASCII." In addition, we could get a carry from the 3rd to 4th bit position (auxiliary carry). There is the possibility of two digit result. i.e., 5 + 5 =10)

ADD; AAA - ASCII adjust after addition. The AAA instruction is used after a binary addition to adjust the result back to proper bcd format. Similarly, the AAS instruction is used to adjust the result after a subtraction.

AAA - example

```
        MOV   AX, 9        ; put 9 into AX
        MOV   BX, 3        ;put 3 into BX (this will generate a carry
when added)
        ADD   AL, BL       ; RESULT = 0Ch
        AAA                ; AH = 01; AL=02;
                           ;SET CARRY
```

There is also AAM, for ASCII ADJUST AFTER MULTIPLY, and AAD; ASCII adjust BEFORE division. Note the adjustment for division is done before the operation.

Packed BCD

Packed bcd has 2 BCD digits per byte. Thus, there are two possible carries, one between the bcd digits in the word, and one out of the word.

The instruction DAA does decimal adjust after addition, and DAS does decimal adjust after subtraction. You are on your own for adjustments for multiply and divide.

Multi-digit BCD numbers can be processed in loops, serial by digit; or converted to integers for the operations on data.

Operations on STRINGS of data

With strings, or sequence of bytes, we can:

- move a string
- scan for a value within a string
- compare strings
- load/store a string
- input/output a string

Strings are what arrays in higher level languages get converted to. They are simple adjacent memory locations that are related. String operations use repeat prefixes. If you think of these operations as processing in a loop, the structure begins to make sense. The repeat prefixes are:

REP- repeat

REPE/REPNE- repeat while equal/not equal

REPZ/REPNZ- repeat while zero/not zero

Setting up a string operations is just like setting up a loop (which they are). The steps are:

- set the direction flag
  - clear = process from low to high addresses
  - set = process from high to low addresses
- put the iteration count in the CX register
- put the source address in the register pair DS:SI
- put the destination address in the register pair ES:DI

Make sure you get the direction flag right. Sometimes, it doesn't matter.

CLD - clear direction flag, to go low to high addresses
STD - set direction flag, to go high to low addresses.

String operations can operate by byte, word, or doubleword. You want to use the largest data size you can, for efficiency. String operations are interruptible.

The repeat prefix REP repeats the string operation, as long as the CX register is not equal to zero.

The REP (condition) repeats the string operation while CX is not equal to zero, AND the condition is true.

The format of the string operation varies. Some have a destination only: SCAS, STOS, INS. Some have source only: LODS, OUTS. Some have both: MOVS, CMPS.

Moving strings can be accomplished by byte, word, or doubleword, from the source to the destination.

Don't be afraid to move a string of bytes as words, or doublewords. Just adjust the count properly, move the odd byte(s) separately if needed.

Example:

```
MOV  CX, COUNT
SHR  CX,1          ; divide by 2
REP  MOVSW         ; move by words
RCL  CX, 1         ; if odd, then cx=1
REP  MOVSB         ; move the final byte if necessary
```

We can also search string for a particular pattern; or compare strings to find the first match or non-match.

We can fill a string with a specified value in each position. We can also store a string in memory.

For loading a value from a string, the string is the source, and the value goes to the AL, AH, or EAX register, depending on the size. Here, we don't use a repeat prefix.

Shifts/rotates – bits go left, bits go right.

When we shift a data element left, it goes toward the MSB. When we shift it right, it goes toward the LSB. The last bit in the direction of the shift goes to the carry flag, and we can make decisions based on the status of that bit.

The shift count is an immediate operand, or contained in the CL register. The maximum shift count is 32. A rotate operation is an end-around carry; no bits fall off the end. There is a difference in arithmetical versus logical shifts. In arithmetic shifts, the sign is preserved.

Shift/rotate types:

- SHL - shift left logical
- SHR - shift right logical
- SAL - shift arithmetic left
- SAR - shift arithmetic right
- ROL - rotate left
- ROR - rotate right
- RCL - rotate left thru carry
- RCR - rotate right thru carry
- SHL - shift logical left (this is the same as the Shift Arithmetic Left)

If we shift left, zero bits are shifted in from the right. Higher order bits are lost (fall off the end, except for a rotate operation).

Shifting to the left one place is equivalent to multiplication by 2, and shifting to the right is like dividing by two (with truncation).

The timing of the shift operations is interesting. In the 80286, the shift timing is 5+n clocks, where n = shift count. In the 80386 and 80486, the shift timing is 3 clocks. Note that the timing is no longer a function of the shift count. This is due to the use of a barrel shifter, a hardware mechanism to shift any number of places in the same number of clocks.

SHR is Shift Logical Right. Zeros come in from the left. The low order bits are shifted out, and lost in the bit bucket. SHR is equivalent to DIV (divide).

SAL is Shift Arithmetic Left. Zero bits come in from the right. High order bits are lost. An overflow indicates that the number has gotten too big to represent.

SAR is Shift Arithmetic Right. The sign bit from before the shift comes in from the left. This operation looks like the integer divide (IDIV), if both operands are positive.

ROL is Rotate Left. Here, each bit goes to next higher bit position. The high order bit goes to the low order position. The last bit rotated is copied to carry flag.

ROR is Rotate Right. Each bit goes to next lower bit position; the low order bit goes to the high order position; the last bit rotated is copied to carry flag.

RCL is rotate left thru carry. It is like an ROL, with an extra bit, CF. We can use this for multi-element (>32 bit) shifts, by storing the high order bit in CF.

RCR is rotate right thru carry. It is like an ROR, with an extra bit, CF. We can use it for multi-element (> 32 bit) shifts, by storing the low order bit in CF.

Shifting multi-word values is relatively straightforward. We would use RCR or RCL with the Carry Flag to link shifts greater than 32 bits. We may need to use the CLC (clear carry flag), CMC (complement carry flag), or STC (set carry flag) to get started.

Double precision (64-bit) shifts are supported on the 80386 and subsequent. These are called SHLD and SHRD.

The Byte Swap operation reverses the order of bytes in a 32 bit register. The 80x86 uses "little endian" storage; the least significant byte of a multi-byte structure is stored at the lowest address. A byte swap converts these to "big endian" format.

Multiply

The Multiply operation can be signed or unsigned. We can do an 8x8, 16x16, or 32x32.

8 x 8 to 16 bits in the AX register.
16 x 16 to 32 bits in the DX:AX register pair.
32 by 32 to 64bits in the EDX:EAX register pair.

One of the factors being multiplied must be in the A register (AL, AX, EAX).

The unsigned multiply is a slow operation. The 80386 and 80486 use an "early out" algorithm to speed this up.

Multiply timings for a 16 bit operand:

8086: 124 to 139 + operand effective address formation time
80286: 24 clocks
80386: 15-28 clocks
80486: 13-42 clocks

The signed multiply operation is called IMUL. It, as the name suggests, gives the proper sign to the result, based on the signs of the factors.

Multiplication can be speeded up by various tricks, that will be discussed later.

Divide

Divide can be signed or unsigned. It is one of the slowest operations; it is to be avoided if at all possible. There are alternatives that can speed up the process if it is necessary.

Divide produces a quotient and a remainder.

divide 16 by 8 bits, to get 8 bit quotient and 8 bit remainder.
divide 32 by 16 bits to get 16 quotient and 16 bit remainder.
divide 64 by 32 bits to get 32 quotient and 32 bit remainder.

The number to be divided (the dividend) is in: AX (16 bits), DX:AX (32 bits), or EDX:EAX (64 bits).

The unsigned divide, DIV, has the property that if the quotient exceeds the capacity of the destination, or division by zero is attempted, interrupt 0 (the divide exception) is generated.

The DIV timing is:

80-172 cycles on 8086
16-40 cycles on 80486

The signed divide format is:

IDIV accumulator

Again, if the quotient exceeds the capacity of the destination, the divide error exception (interrupt 0) is generated. The instruction timing is: 19 to 44 cycles, on the 80486.

To divide a 16-bit word by another 16-bit word, you need to sign-extend the 16-bit dividend to 32-bit, and then do the divide operation (signed or unsigned).

Faster Math

There are many tricks to avoid the time-consuming operations by exploiting fore-knowledge or characteristics of the parameters.

By using table lookups we can trade space for time. The values are pre-calculated, and put in a table in memory. Then a particularly computationally costly function value can be obtained in a simple access to the table. The calculations are done once, offline.

There is a lot of redundancy in the instruction set. There are trade-offs in different methods of doing something – check instruction timings.

Multiply and divide by constants is easily accomplished by shifts. In the simplest case, multiplication or division by powers of two, can be done entirely by shifts.

A multiply by 2 can take 74-81 clocks. The equivalent shift would take 2 clocks.

Multiplying or dividing, by sums of powers of 2's involves several shifts, and storage of intermediate products.

For example, to multiply by 10, factor $10 = 8 + 2$. The multiply is accomplished with a shift to get the value of the item times two, a store operation, and a shift another 2 places (to get x 8), and then an addition.

To multiply by 13, we factor $13 = 16 – 3 = 16 – 2 - 1$. We need several shifts and adds, but this still takes less time than a multiply.

We can generally do this with powers of 2 +/- 1 3, 5, 7, 9, etc.

To multiply by	factor	shifts and adds
1	1	null operation
2	2	shift 1
3	2+1	shift 1 and add
4	4	shift 2
5	4+1	shift 2 and add
6	4+2	shift, store, shift, add
7	4+2+1	shift, store, shift, add, add
8	8	shift 3
9	8+1	shift 3 and add
10	8+2	shift 1,store, shift 2 more, add
etc.		

Multiply by ten example code:

```
MUL10      MACRO      FACTOR
           MOV        AX, FACTOR      ; grab the multiplier
           SHL        AX,1            ; multiply it by two
           MOV        BX, AX          ; save that
           SHL        AX, 1           ; multiply it by 4
           SHL        AX,1            ; multiply it by 8
           ADD        AX,BX           ; add the *8+*2=*10
           ENDM
```

Divide by 512 example:

```
DIV512     MACRO      DIVIDEND
           MOV        AX, DIVIDEND    ; grab the dividend
           SHR        AX,1            ; shift it right by 1 (i.e.,
divide by 2)
           XCHG       AL,AH           ; same as shift right by 8,
divide by 256
           CBW                        ;clear upper byte; zeros in the
upper 8 bits.
           ENDM
```

Besides knowing whether the division operation preserves the sign, we need to know if the result is rounded or truncated. With DIV and SHR, positive numbers are truncated toward zero.

If memory is a less expensive resource than time, you can pre-compute a function, and store the values in a table in memory. A function call to get a value takes one basic access time. The input variable becomes the index into the table. The more accuracy that is required, the larger is the table. This can be used for the trigonometric, transcendental, and other complex functions.

In binary computers, we do not necessarily need to convert angles to decimal operate to operate on them. Recall that our angles are decimal, but we use 360 degrees, or 2 X Pi radians because of the Babylonians. In binary, we can use binary radians, where we divide the circle into 256 or 1024 parts. Calculations can be done on these binary radian ("brad") values quickly and efficiently, and the final conversion to decimal degrees or angles is done at the end of the calculation, if required.

If we use the floating point unit to do trigonometric calculations for us, the numbers are assumed to be in decimal degrees, in floating point representation.

The sine of an angle can be pre-calculated and saved in a table, for example. The size of the table will depend on the desired accuracy. For a full 360 degree range, and an accuracy of 1 degree, we only need 90 elements in the table. We can exploit the symmetries of the sine function, and use a few lines of code (8, for example) to determine the quadrant the angle is in, do the lookup, and adjust accordingly. We can creatively reuse the sine table for a cosine table as well by using the trigonometric identities. This would add one line of code, and utilize the same data table. The angle is used as an index into the table, which takes about 3 lines of code.

These same techniques can be used for most functions where the cost of calculation is high. We only need to calculate the values once.

We can also use tables for code. We can build a table of jump address targets, and use an index to the table to generate a structure similar to the "CASE" statement in some higher order languages. It is important to do range checking on the index to the table, so that we don't jump to strange and unanticipated locations in the code.

Interrupt architecture

The 80x86 architecture has a single interrupt request line, and a corresponding acknowledge line. Interrupts can be prioritized by external hardware (the interrupt priority controller) up to 256 different ones. The PC architecture has 8, the AT architecture has 15. Intel's interrupt controller is the 8259 chip, priority interrupt controller. It manages 8 interrupts and is cascade-able, using 1 input to chain to another device. Interrupt with the highest priority are recognized first.

External interrupt sequence of events:

- Processor is happily executing instructions, when…
- A nasty external device signals for attention on the interrupt request line. If the interrupts are enabled,...
- The processor completes the current instruction, and signals acknowledgment on ACK line.
- The interrupting device puts an 8-bit code on the lower 8 lines of the databus.
- The processor reads this code, multiplies it by 4, and jumps to that location.
- Hopefully, this gets us to an interrupt service routine.

Interrupt vector table (IVT)

In real mode, the IVT is in the lower 1024 locations of RAM. It is a table of addresses. Each entry is 4 bytes, the new CS and the new IP register contents. Who sets this up? It is the operating system's responsibility. There must be a valid entry in each location, otherwise an interrupt might go off into never-never land.

Interrupt by software

INT xx is the interrupt instruction, which causes a synchronous interrupt. It is repeatable and cannot be masked. It can generate any possible interrupt, including those reserved to hardware conditions (divide by 0, for example). Execution of the instruction kicks off a sequence just like an external interrupt would. This provides a convenient inter-process communication mechanism. It is used by the BIOS (interrupts 00 to 1F) and the DOS (interrupts 20 to 3F).

Interrupts from external sources

External interrupts are asynchronous, by definition. The processor never knows when they will happen. The timing is controlled by the external I/O device.

Variable length instructions in the architecture make it hard to predict exact interrupt response times. They can be bounded, however. Remember that the lengthy string instructions are interrupt-able.
The priority of external interrupts is generally higher than that of the executing program. The Operating system software sets and manages priorities.

Exceptions are interrupts caused by internal condition, usually the result of instruction execution. They are synchronous to the execution of instructions.. Examples are:

> Fault - reported before the instruction is executed.
> Trap - reported during execution of the instruction
> Abort - severe error. No restart possible.

We can choose to ignore interrupts by software, all except the non-maskable interrupt.

If we use the instruction, CLI - clear interrupt flag, the processor will not recognize maskable interrupts. We really want to have the interrupts locked out for as short a time as possible, because the interrupts are a necessary part of system I/O. We can also use the instruction STI - set interrupt flag, for the processor to continue to recognize and respond to interrupts. Interrupt handling is transparent to the running program, and it leaves the processor in the same state as before the interrupt occurs.

An Interrupt service routine (ISR) is a small subroutine that responds to the request for service by the external device. It is terminated by an IRET instruction, the return from interrupt. This gets the returns address off the stack, and returns to the point where the cpu was executing, before the interrupt occurred. A lot of ISR's are written in assembly for speed. Writing hardware-specific ISR's is something of an art form. It requires in-depth knowledge of the hardware on both sides of the interface.

The INTO instruction generates software interrupt 4, if the Overflow flag (OF) is set.

For simultaneous interrupts, there are defined rules of priority. These depend on the specific processor, and can be found in the manufacturer's data sheet..

Processor-reserved interrupts

Some of the 256 possible interrupts in the x86 architecture are reserved by the chip manufacturer for specific purposes. In the PC board architecture, more interrupts are reserved for specific I/O functions, such as the serial and parallel ports, and the floppy and disk drives. Some of these have been redefined over the years as hardware has evolved. We may no longer need the cassette drive interface for storing data, but we do now have a mouse. (trivia question: what is the name for the smallest resolvable motion of a mouse? It's a "mickey." Really.)

Intel, the chip manufacturer, reserved the interrupts 00 thru 1Fx, but not all are defined.

The processor-defined interrupts:

    00 = divide error
    01 = single step
    02 = NMI (non-maskable interrupt)
    06 = invalid opcode
    08 = double fault
    0D = general protection fault
    0E = page fault

An exception occurs after the execution of an instruction. The resulting flag is cleared, the single-step handler is executed in normal mode. It resets the flag before exit. The 80386 and subsequent have built-in debugging features, relying on interrupts.

NMI

The non-maskable interrupt is the highest priority external interrupt; it cannot be masked by software. This feature came about because of an oversight in earlier processor design. It the hardware allowed the software to mask all of the interrupts, there is the possibility of getting into a state that you could not get out of, except for turning off the power. Since that time, all processors have an interrupt that cannot be ignored by the software.

Invalid opcode interrupt

On the 80286 and subsequent, this signals an attempt to execute a bit pattern not defined by Intel as a valid opcode. Before this, the case could happen, with unpredictable results. 8086/8088 chips made by different manufacturers did different things when these undefined bit patterns were executed. It was an exciting time for programmers. In the Intel 80286, the $D4_{16}$ opcode set the AL register to the value of the carry. Undocumented opcodes were generally not supported in the assembler with mnemonics, but could be defined directly in hex. With the invalid opcode trap, undocumented op codes became obsolete. This is interrupt 06_{16} in the Intel scheme of things.

Double Fault interrupt

This is an exception during the handling of an exception. This is very bad. It means we had two protection violations during the execution of a single instruction. The processor goes to shutdown, and we need to RESET. This is an obscure case that shouldn't happen if the operating system is on its toes. (Do operating systems have toes?)

Advanced double fault interrupt

It just gets better on the 80386 and subsequent processors. They became smarter (more clever) in unraveling multiple faults. There are now two categories: benign faults and contributory faults. Some of these double faults are recoverable. This is the operating system's responsibility.

General protection fault interrupt

This is mostly associated with protected mode. It signals an attempt to write into a read-only segment. This can be caused by somehow treating the stack as read-only, or treating the data as execute-only. This is an operating system issue.

Page fault interrupt

On the 80386 and later, this signals an error detected during address translation where a page is not present in memory. This happens a lot in virtual memory management, and is handled by the operating system.

Pseudo operations

Pseudos, also called directives, do not generate code, but supply information to the assembler program. They are grouped in with the opcodes in the input to the assembler.

examples: TITLE
SEGMENT
DW (define word)
DB (define byte)

For all of these, refer to the reserved word list for the particular assembler. The names of these pseudos cannot also be used for labels, they are reserved words.

Comments in assembler follow a semicolon.

example:

; this is a comment

MOV AH,02H ; this is also

Labels

The rules for labels are assembler-dependent, but they are generally a maximum of 31 characters. They can use letters (upper & lower case), numbers, special characters such as "? . @ _ $" . Labels give us the ability to associate words of meaning to us to locations in the program. There are Near and Far labels in the 80x86 scheme of things. A near label refers to a location in the same 64k segment, and is 16 bits in size. A far label refers to a location anywhere in the address space, and has two 16-bit parts. During the first pass of the assembler program through the user code, all of the label names are collected and put into a table. Later, these will be assigned memory locations.

Changes in the flow of control are important in the program. We usually don't run through the code in a single path from top to bottom. The use of data-dependent branches is a powerful feature. Standard control constructs from high-level languages translate to assembly easily.

Addressing modes on the 8086

Segment registers in the x86 architecture select a 64k byte block (addressed by 16 bits) out of a 1 megabyte address space (provided by 20 address lines), in real mode.

Segments start on 16 byte boundaries (because segments are multiplied by 16, or shifted left by 4 bits).These are called paragraphs.

There are 64k different segment starting addresses; in each, the 4 low order address bits are zero. Segments may overlap, but it complicates things.

Effective Address Calculation

This section is unique to the Intel x86 architecture. The x86 does not have a flat directly addressed space like most processors. It is a complicated scheme, so pay attention.

The Bus Interface Unit (BIU) Segment Base Registers

The processor can address 1,048,576 bytes of memory and requires 20 address lines in real mode. The internal registers of the processor are 16 bits wide and can only generate 64k different addresses. The designers of the x86 architecture decided to have each 64k segment start on a paragraph address. A paragraph address is always a multiple of 16.

Notice that the 4 lower bits of the paragraph address are always 0; therefore, the paragraph address can be expressed as a sixteen bit binary number with the 4 lower bits implied. The paragraph address of the 64k segment is stored in a segment base register located in the BIU.

The 8086/88 had four segment base registers called the code segment (CS), data segment (DS), extra segment (ES), and the stack segment (SS). When an instruction references memory, the paragraph address (shifted left by 4 bits) of the proper segment is added to 16-bit address provided by the instruction. The result is the 20 bit address in the physical memory. The 16-bit address, provided by the instruction, is called the OFFSET within the segment or the effective address.

119

As an example, suppose an instruction is referencing location 1234h in the data segment. Further, let us assume the paragraph register for the DS segment contains 2001h. The physical address, within memory, is calculated as follows:

```
paragraph register shifted left 4 bits = 20010h
plus offset of data within segment =     1234h
                                        -------
physical address in memory=             21244h
```

The virtual address is expressed as XXXX:YYYY, where XXXX is the contents of the segment base register and YYYY is the offset within the segment. The virtual address of the above is: 2001:1234 SEG:OFF.

$$SEG * 16 + OFF = ADD$$

Example: 2001:1234=>21244 hex

```
20010          ;shifted left by 4 bits, lsb's = 0
+1234
------------
21234
```

Memory Segments

Recall that there are four segment registers in the x86 architecture, with default assumptions as to which segments they are pointing to.

The CS or code segment register points to the area where instructions to be executed are stored. The IP or instruction pointer contains the offset address within the code segment of the instruction to be executed next.

The DS or data segment points to the area where data references will be made. The DS is also used to specify the source for string manipulation instructions. The offset address is provided by the instruction.

The SS or stack segment points to the area where the stack will be placed. The offset is provided by the Stack Pointer.

The ES or extra segment may be used for data, or destination operands of string manipulation operations. In the 386 and subsequent, there are also the FS and GS segment registers.

Code addressing modes

Code addressing is much simpler. The CS register points to the code segment, and the Instruction Pointer (or, Program Counter) provided by the hardware provides the offset. Only a direct address is used. This will be the address of the next instruction to be executed, as automatically calculated by the hardware. Since the instructions are variable length, we need the calculation.

Data Addressing Modes

Data addressing is more complicated. An instruction usually specifies a source and a destination. These can be registers or memory or the stack. In different modes of addressing the address is known (or, resolved) at different times. Some of the modes are complicated, and little used. They can simplify the addressing of complex data structures, such as multiple-dimensioned arrays.

Format:

Instruction Destination, Source

where destination = memory or register
source = memory or register or immediate

Details of Addressing modes:

Register to register addressing is straightforward; not all combinations are valid. You need to check the instruction syntax.

Immediate to register or memory has a value calculated at assembly time, and included as part of the instruction. No string constants greater than 2 characters are allowed.

In direct addressing, the contents of the symbolic memory address are source and destination; and the value is calculated at load time.

In indirect addressing, the register contents are considered as an address; the value is calculated at run time. The indirect modes use the BX, BP, SI, or DI registers. Memory operands default to the data segment, except when BP used as a base register, when the stack segment is assumed.

In Base + displacement mode, a fixed displacement is added to the address. This could be an offset in a table, for example.

In Base + index + displacement mode, the contents of a register + the contents of an index register plus a fixed displacement form the address.

The Segment Override Specification is used to access data in a different segment than the default one.

example:

MOV AX , ES : [BX]

A word within the extra segment at an offset equal to the contents of BX will be moved into register AX. Recall that the Extra segment is a Data-type segment.

Program Flow

JUMPS

Jumps implement changes in the flow of a program. They can be unconditional or conditional. The unconditional jump is always taken; it is the GOTO. The conditional Jump depends on the result of a previous calculation in the program, as contained in the flags register.

LOOPS

Loops are control structures that are executed for a number of iterations times, or are executed until a calculated condition is met.

TEST BITS & JUMP

In terms of jumps, we must consider the concept of distance to the referenced label. This is the number of memory bytes (the difference in addresses) of the referring and the referenced items. From the current instruction, labels may be in one of three distance categories:

Short   -128 to + 127 bytes away

Near   -32768 to 32,767 bytes away, but in the same segment

Far   in a different segment

A short reference only needs 1 byte of address specifier, and a near reference needs 2 bytes. A far reference needs 4 bytes. Two hold the offset, and two hold a new segment address.

A J U M P does a transfer unconditionally to a specified address:

syntax:

J M P operand

where operand := register or address

The register contents or address value is used with CS to form a new effective address, which is then used to update the IP register.

Examples:

J M P Label1

Label1:   ; jump target

This instruction generates 3 bytes of code, as Label1 is a forward reference, and the assembler must assume a near jump (within the same segment, but greater than 127 bytes away). If you know that the target address is within 128 bytes, you can force a short jump:

J M P S H O R T Label1

This has the effect of generating a 2 byte (instead of 3 byte) instruction that executes slightly faster. This will also generate a warning message. If the target is more than 127 bytes away, an error message will be generated. For backward (previously defined) references, this procedure is not required.

In the case of far jumps case, the target address is in another segment, and a 5 byte instruction is generated:

J M P FAR PTR Label1

The PTR (pointer) operator forces the operand Label1 to have the type FAR. A total of 4 bytes is required to specify the new segment (2 bytes) and the offset (2 bytes).

Conditional jumps involve a two -step process: test the condition, jump if true; continue if false.

Syntax:

       CMP   operand 1, operand 2
       J XX   address

where:

operand 1 := register or memory
operand 2 := register, memory, or immediate
XX   := condition
address   := short

To use near or far conditional jumps, either reverse the sense of the test and use a near or far conditional jump, or use the conditional jump to jump to a near or far unconditional jump instruction.

LOOPS are used for iteration control.

Syntax:

       LOOP x Address

means:

       $CX = CX - 1$

if $CX = 0$, fall thru, else jump

There are also forms that allow us to terminate loop early. The loop involves short jumps only, so there is a maximum size.

The Loop instruction is placed at the end of the loop; it jumps back to the beginning. This means there is at least one iteration through the loop. We need to initialize the repeat count before entering the loop.

Subroutines

Subroutines provide for a transfer of control to a different piece of code, with a way to get back. The mechanisms are:

    CALL SUB1

    SUB1 PROC NEAR   ;define the subroutine procedure
    . . .
    . . . code goes here
    . . .
        RET   ;return
    SUB1 ENDP   ; end of subroutine procedure definition

At the subroutine CALL, the return location is pushed on the stack by the CPU. (you did set up the stack, right?) At RET, the return location is popped off the stack and place in the program counter. This gets the program back to where it was. Within the same segment, we only need the offset (16 bits) address. Between different segments, we need the new segment address (16 bits) and the offset (16 bits).

Macro

The Macro gives us a method to assign a symbolic name to a block of code. We can then reference the code block by name in the source file. At assembly time, the macro is expanded. This is a text processing function done by the assembler. When the macro name is encountered later in the code by the assembler, it is replaced by the previously defined code block. We might think of this as an in-line subroutine without the overhead of linkage.

Parameters may be passed to macros. Macros may contain labels (these are assembler-generated to make them unique). A macro definition must precede its use. Macro statements are not assembled when encountered, only when used. Details on syntax are assembler-specific.

Modular design

As we get better at programming, we develop a program style. It is important to develop a programming mindset; specifically, how will I debug this? This is facilitated by document at development time. We also want to define data structures first, then the processing, or operations on those structures. In addition, if shortcuts are required for speed or space, you need to document your assumptions, and your violations. If you get too clever, others won't be able to figure out your code, and neither will you, later.

X86 Boot sequence

How does the processor get started? Upon power on, a special hardware circuit generates a RESET signal to the processor. RESET is a special type of interrupt. The RESET signal takes the processor to a known state. All of the registers will contain known values, defined by the manufacturer. Specifically, the program counter contains a specific address for program start. For the Intel x86 architecture, this is at the top of memory. Thus, we need a Jump instruction at the top of memory, to a bootloader routine. This can be implemented by having some non-volatile memory at the top of the address space.

The 8086 reset

Hit the red button. What does this do? Well, it causes a special interrupt to the processor.
Several registers are set to particular values:

```
IP  = 0000h    ; instruction pointer
CS = FFFFh    ; Code Segment register
DS = ES = SS = 0000h        ; data, extra, and stack segment
```
registers.

After reset on the 8086, the processor accesses an address 16 bytes below the top of memory, fetches the instruction from there, and executes it.

What is 16 bytes below the top of memory? Well, that's the key question. The Operating System, specifically the BIOS, is responsible for putting a proper value there. Since the address is only 16 bytes below the top of memory, we can't put much of a program there, but we can put a Jump instruction to anywhere else in memory.

So, what's there? Again, the Operating System is responsible for putting a program there, that does whatever we want to do after a RESET. Do a clean-up, restart a program, etc.

If there isn't something valid in those locations, the process still continues, but the results may be less than desirable.

The BIOS ROM

At the high end of memory, we need a persistent copy of the code that will be executed in the case of a reset. This was accomplished by putting the program in ROM, and putting it there in the address space. Since the 8086 could only address one megabyte of memory, this simply put an upper limit to the useable memory. And, at that time, system didn't have (couldn't afford) a megabyte of memory anyway. With later processors being able to address larger memory spaces, the BIOS ROM stuck at the first megabyte of memory was a pain. It remains that way.

At the low end of memory 0000h, we need some RAM, some memory to read and write. Advanced processor reset is similar to that of the 8086, in that it initializes in real mode. This because the BIOS is not compatible with Protected mode.

The contents of this memory has come to be called the BIOS, the basic input output system. It does hardware initialization, some testing (POST), and has a boot loader. The boot loader is a piece of code just smart enough to load the rest of the operating system from files on a secondary storage device, such as a disk or flash memory. The process is called, pulling yourself up by your bootstraps. The default loader gets some code from a known location on the storage device, loads it into memory, and jumps to the code. This rudimentary loader can then load the operating systems (or, perhaps, one of several operating systems) from the storage medium.

Power On Self Test, or POST, executes a rudimentary series of tests of the system components. This is incredibly difficult, conceptually, because the computer hardware tests itself. Assumptions must be made about minimal functionality. The POST part of the BIOS function is probably the most interesting part.

CPUid instruction

An interesting exercise to see if we understand the hardware, is to write a program to determining the processor hardware we are running on. Actually, with the introduction of the CPUid instruction with the Pentium processor in 1993, it is very easy. We just ask the processor what it is. Before the Pentium, we had to make use of processor idiosyncrasies of the processors, executed in the right order, to figure this out. It was also possible to identify which company made the processor.

This was such an interesting problem that I once assigned it in class to a very advanced student, in lieu of homeworks and exams. He completed the assignment, and handed in a well-documented piece of code, that explained how he would systematically test the underlying hardware that the code was executing on.

Today, code reads the processor type to see what series of optimizations should be applied. Optimizations for one implementation may be exactly the wrong thing to do for other implementations.

LoadALL instruction

The LOADALL instruction (OF, 05) was an undocumented opcode introduced with the 80286. There is a completely different LOADALL (0F 07) for the 80386, and after that, the instruction was discontinued. In the early processors, not all bit codes were valid instructions, and the ones that were not valid instructions were not necessarily ignored. Some non-valid bit patterns actually did something useful. However, these bit patterns would not necessarily work with X86 processors from other manufacturers. Now, un-implemented instruction codes default to an interrupt.

The LOADALL is a deliberate instruction, kept out of the general instruction list. Its function was to load all of the CPU internal registers at once. This allowed cpu states not generally allowed in the X86 programming model. It required 195 machine cycles to complete, and used a 102 byte area in memory starting at address 0800_{16} to hold the entire set of processor state information. It was a backdoor method of getting out of protected mode without a reset on the 80286. The 80386 Loadall was undocumented and not supported by Intel. The hex code was OF 07. It loaded a 204 byte area pointed to by the ES:EDI register pair into all of the internal registers. That covered the entire internal execution state information.

LOADALL was used by utilities to gain access to additional memory without leaving REAL mode. This was used by the utility HIMEM.SYS. It would also allow a 16-bit protected mode. This was used in digital Researches Concurrent DOS 286 operating system. LOADALL could also enter a real mode with paging support on 386's.

With full protected mode operating systems, the LOADALL instruction was not needed.

Self-Modifying code in x86

First, understand, self-modifying code is evil. You should never do it. It is all Von Neumann's fault, because he erased the line between the code and the data.

Actually, the assembler writes "data" into the code area. What we are talking about here is a running program modifying itself as it runs. Sometimes that seems like a clever way around a tough problem, but it is extremely difficult to debug if something goes wrong.

Code can modify itself during an initialization phase based on a menu of input parameters. This eliminates a lot of conditionals, and reducing program size. We can also have a program that modifies itself as it runs, overwriting instructions with new ones. Essentially, we have dynamic instruction creation.

Some higher order languages allow for code to be modified, while others (Python, JavaScript) allow programs to create new code at run time, which is then executed.

Self-modifying code has been used to conceal such features as copy protection, or viruses or malware. Some operating systems control the write-ability of the code segment.

In systems with cache, writing to memory might actually only be writing to the cache, which has a finite lifetime.

Trivia Question: Which instruction in the x86 architecture assembles to 00 00 00 00 00 00 00 ?

   Answer: ADD [BX+SI], AL

Protected mode

This discussion is specific to the Intel x86 architecture.

Protected Mode on the 80286

The DOS operating system is not compatible with Protected Mode. One can enter Protected Mode from DOS, but not necessarily get back. Protected Mode was introduced on the 80286 to extend the addressing capabilities of the x86 architecture beyond one megabyte. The 8086 native mode is called REAL mode.

Protected mode on the 80286 is of some academic interest only, because there is no way of returning to real mode, except by a hardware reset. It is referred to by some as virtual mode. The concept was that setup would be done in real mode after reset, and the system would transition to Protected mode for subsequent operations.

Operating systems such as OS/2, UNIX, linux, bsd, and Windows take advantage of Protected Mode's advanced features. For example, multiple copies of DOS can run under UNIX, sharing system resources transparently. The 640k memory barrier is artificial.

The 80286 and 80386 enter real mode at reset. This mode is comparable with 8086. By software, you can command an entry to protected mode. On the 80286, it isn't easy to get back to real mode via software. On the 80386 and subsequent processors, you can.

In protected mode, you have all the features of real mode, plus:

- Virtual addressing

- More memory addressable (16 Mb vs. 1 Mb on the 80286)

- Protection mechanisms for operating system software

Protected Mode offers advanced features that can be used by operating systems to support multitasking.

Virtual Addressing

The physical address space is what you have to work with. The virtual address space is what you pretend to have to work with. The processor does the dynamic mapping between virtual and physical address. This memory management technique is called address translation, and requires additional overhead on each memory access.

On 80286, physical address is 2^{24} = 16 Megabytes, and the virtual address is 2^{30} = 1 gigabyte.

With virtual memory, you can write applications that assume you have 1 gigabyte available, and rely on the operating system to swap the correct virtual memory pages into and out of the existing physical memory. This, of course, takes time.

Memory beyond 640k without protected mode is possible, but it involved a lot of overhead. First, we need to look at memory classifications.

In conventional memory, there are 10 segments of 64 k each - "more than any programmer could ever need." The 640k barrier is at $A0000_h$, with the display mapped memory being placed there.

Extended memory is memory beyond 1 megabyte on the 80286 and subsequent. It needs a memory manager program, such as himem.sys.

Expanded memory uses gaps between 640k and 1 megabyte. It maps up to 16 megabytes of memory into these gaps, using a manager, written to the LIMM specification (Lotus-Intel-Microsoft). It was used for DOS applications, not for Windows, which has its own manager program.

Virtual memory

We can use hard disk space used as memory, in the form of a swap file. Disk memory is much less expensive than semiconductor memory, but much slower as well. The virtual memory is mapped through regular memory. In additional to the penalty of the speed, there is extensive software overhead as well in the translation process. Thrashing refers to

134

the scenario where the system is caught up in swapping memory, without getting anything else done.

The upper memory area is the 384k above 640k, in the DOS world. There is system hardware mapping in this area, for example, for the display adapters, the BIOS in the pc architecture, and BASIC in ROM in the IBM pc architecture. Unused memory gaps are called upper memory blocks (UMB).

The high memory area is the first 64k of extended memory. Through a quirk of the addressing scheme, this can be addressed in real mode.

To understand the physical address calculation process in protected mode, we should first review the Physical Address Calculation in real mode. There is a 16-bit segment specifier plus a 16-bit offset. The address is in two 16-bit parts, a segment and an offset. We shift the segment part over to the left by four bits (or, equivalently, multiply it by 16), and add the offset. We get a 20-bit result.

Physical address = segment * 16 + offset

This provides a 20-bit physical address which spans $2^{20} = 1$ megabyte of address space.

(now it gets complicated)

In protected mode, there is a 16-bit segment selector plus a 16-bit offset to yield a 32-bit virtual address. The virtual address is what the running program uses. The system converts the virtual address to a physical address (in real time) that goes out over the memory bus to the system's memory. There is more virtual memory than real memory. The bookkeeping is handled by the system, partially in hardware and partially in software.

Along with protected mode, Intel introduced the ring model of privilege, modeled on the Unix approach. There are 4 layers, where the innermost is the most trusted, and the outermost is the user program.

The base address of the segment in memory is not calculated by multiplying the segment specifier by 16, but rather by indexing a table in memory. This table, previously set up by the program or operating system, is called the descriptor table. It contains more than just the address translation information.

The Selector Table contains entries called selectors. Selectors contain three fields:

> The Requested Privilege Level (RPL),
> The Table Indicator (TI), and
> Index (I)

The RPL field does not concern address translation, but is used by the operating system to implement privilege level protection. It is a number 0-3. The intent is to prevent a less-privileged program from accessing data from a more privileged one.

The TI field specifies the table to be used by the Global Descriptor Table (TI = 0) or the Local Descriptor Table (TI = 1). These are data structures residing in memory, and set up by the operating system. Global Descriptor Tables are pointed to by the Global Descriptor Tables registers. The Descriptor Table Registers can be read and written by specific instructions; the GDTR by the instructions LGDT and SGDT, and the LDTR by LLDT and SLDT. On the 80286, there is one GDT, and each task can have its own LDT.

The Index is a pointer into the table. Descriptors are 8 bytes long. The index item is a 24-bit address for the corresponding segment (on the 80286. 32-bits on 80386 and subsequent).

The 24-bit address obtained from the selector table look-up is added to the 16 bit offset to form a 24-bit physical address. Overflows are ignored, thus addresses wrap around.

If TI = 0 (GDT) and Index = 0, this is the null selector. If it is used for address translation, it results in an exception.

The index field is 13 bits, so a descriptor table can have up to 2^{13} descriptors. Each describes a segment of 2^{16} bytes. So, each task can have a private memory space of 2^{29} bytes. A segment is 64k bytes on the 80286. On the 80386 and subsequent, with 32-bit offset addresses, the virtual address space is 2^{46} bytes.

Segment descriptors are located in the descriptor table. They consist or two parts, a base address and a limit. They contain status and control information for access. They provide a link between a task, and a segment in memory.

Memory descriptors specify a type, code or data. Code is executable, data can be read-only or read-write. These distinctions are imposed by the data structure; the memory is Von Neumann, and read-write. The Type field differs for code and data. The code segment can be accessed, can be readable or not, and is conforming or not. The data segment can be accessed, writable or not, and expands up or expands down (like a stack).

The access byte contains an indicator bit about whether the segment is physically present in memory or not.

Swapping and Mapping

The maximum amount of physical memory is 16 megabytes, so disks are used to hold other virtual pages that are mapped into and out of physical RAM by the operating system.

Further complication of protected mode includes the fact that the math coprocessors ('287, '387) also have a protected mode, and interrupt servicing in Protected Mode involves an Interrupt descriptor table, interrupt gates, and call gates.

In protected mode, calling and jumping involve an inter-segment FAR call through a call gate. The privilege level of the caller is checked against the privilege of the called program (in the gate descriptor). It the level is not good enough, a general protection fault (INT $0D_h$) is generated.

Before entering protected mode, all of the necessary data structures such as the descriptors tables, must be properly set up. This is an operating system function. Then the LMSW (load machine status word) instruction is executed, with the PE (protection enable) bit = 1. Simple. BUT.... First, the instruction queue must be flushed. This is because the instructions were fetched in real mode, but are to be executed (now) in protected mode. How do we flush the queue? Simply do a short jump to the very next location beyond the jump. Jumps force an instruction queue flush. The astute reader will notice that the short jump is fetched in real mode and executed in protected mode, but that's ok – it works.

Exiting protected mode on the 80286 required a RESET or the Loadall instruction. On the 80386 and subsequent, return to real mode simply requires resetting the PE bit by instruction.

Another concept that came along with Protected Mode was that of tasks. There can be many tasks in the system, only one running at a time. These are controlled by the operating system (itself a task) with the TSS- Task State Segment structure. This contains the task state (essentially, register contents). The processor has a task register for the currently running task that is user-visible. There are also pointers (not visible) to the TSS. The Task register is loaded and stored with the LTR/STR instructions. The TSS descriptor looks like a descriptor that we have talked about, but has an idle/busy bit. Tasks are not re-entrant under this scheme.

The Task gate descriptor is an indirect, protected way of accessing a task. It resides in the GDT. A task that does not have enough privilege to use the TSS descriptor can call another task through a gate in the LDT.

Task switching is managed by the operating system, and involves controlled calls and jumps. Interrupts are also managed.

Virtual-86 mode was introduced in the 80386 as an 8086 emulation mode. The 80386 can implement multiple 8086 environments running "simultaneously" in protected environments. These are virtual machines. There is some minor differences in how memory above 1 megabyte is treated.

Page level protection was implemented on the 80386 and subsequent processors. This involves a user/supervisor bit, and supervisor write protection. Paging uses smaller, fixed-size memory blocks. Segmentation uses larger, variable size blocks. Page mode is enabled with a single bit. It can be used with segmentation, as an additional layer of protection, with additional overhead. Pages in the x86 are 4096 bytes, at an address divisible by 1000_h. The page directory and tables are used to control the pages. CR3, the control register, has the page frame address or the page directory in the high order 20 bits. The page directory can hold 1 million entries. Each entry is a pointer to a page table. The page table contains pointers to physical memory.

Floating Point

This section describes the floating point number representation, and explains when it is used, and why. Floating point is an old computer technique for gaining dynamic range in scientific and engineering calculations, at the cost of accuracy. First, we look at fixed point, or integer, calculations to see where the limitations are. Then, we'll examine how floating point helps expand the limits.

In a finite word length machine, there is a tradeoff between dynamic range and accuracy in representation. The value of the most significant bit sets the dynamic range because the effective value of the most positive number is infinity. The value of the least significant bit sets the accuracy, because a value less than the LSB is zero. And, the MSB and the LSB are related by the word length.

In any fixed point machine, the number system is of a finite size. For example, in 18 bit word, we can represent the positive integers from 0 to $2^{18}-1$, or 262,143. A word of all zeros = 0, and a word of all ones = 262,143. I'm using 18 bits as an example because it's not too common. There's nothing magic about 8, 16, or 32 bit word sizes.

If we want to use signed numbers, we must give up one bit to represent the sign. Of course, giving up one bit halves the number of values available in the representation. For a signed integer in an 18 bit word, we can represent integers from + to - 131,072. Of course, zero is a valid number. Either the positive range or the negative range must give up a digit so we can represent zero. For now, let's say that in 18 bits, we can represent the integers from -131,072 to 131,071.

There are several ways of using the sign bit for representation. We can have a sign-magnitude format, a 1's complement, or a two's complement representation. Most computers use the 2's complement representation. This is easy to implement in hardware. In this format, to form the negative of a number, complement all of the bits (1->0, 0->1), and add 1 to the least significant bit position. This is equivalent to forming the 1's complement, and then adding one. One's complement format has the problem that there are two representations of zero, all bits 0 and all bits 1. The hardware has to know that these are equivalent. This added complexity has led to 1's complement schemes falling out of use in favor of 2's complement. In two's complement, there is one representation of zero (all bits zero), and one less positive number, than the negatives. (Actually, since zero is considered positive, there are the same number. But, the negative numbers have more range.) This is easily illustrated for 3-bit numbers, and can be extrapolated to any other fixed length representation.

Remember that the difference between a signed and an unsigned number lies in our interpretation of the bit pattern.

Interpretation of 4-bit patterns

Up to this point we have considered the bit patterns to represent integer values, but we can also insert an arbitrary binary point (analogous to the decimal point) in the word. For integer representations, we have assumed the binary point to lie at the right side of the word, below the LSB. This gives the LSB a weight of 2^0, or 1, and the msb has a weight of 2^{16}. (The sign bit is in the 2^{17} position). Similarly, we can use a fractional representation where the binary point is assumed to lie between the sign bit and the MSB, the MSB has a weight of 2^{-1}, and the LSB has a weight of 2^{-17}. For these two cases we have:

The MSB sets the range, the LSB sets the accuracy, and the LSB and MSB are related by the word length. For cases between these extremes, the binary point can lie anywhere in the word, or for that matter, outside the word. For example, if the binary point is assumed to lie 2 bits to the right of the LSB, the LSB weight, and thus the precision, is 2^2. The MSB is then 2^{19}. We have gained dynamic range at the cost of precision. If we assume the binary point is to the left of the MSB, we must be careful to ignore the sign, which does not have an associated digit weight. For an assumed binary point 2 bit positions to the right of the MSB, we have a MSB weight of 2^{-3}, and an LSB weight of 2^{-20}. We have gained precision at the cost of dynamic range.

It is important to remember that the computer does not care where we assume the binary point to be. It simply treats the numbers as integers during calculations. We overlay the bit weights and the meanings.

A 16-bit integer can represent the values between -16384 to 16384

A 32-bit integer can represent the values between $-2*10^9$ to $2*10^9$

A short real number has the range 10^{-37} to 10^{38} in 32 bits.

A long real number has the range 10^{-307} to 10^{308} in 64 bits

We can get 18 decimal (BCD) digits packed into 80 bits.

To add or subtract scaled values, they must have the same scaling factor; they must be commensurate. If the larger number is normalized, the smaller number must be shifted to align it for the operation. This may have the net result of adding or subtracting zero, as bits fall out the right side of the small word. This is like saying that 10 billion + .00001 is approximately 10 billion, to 13 decimal places of accuracy.

In multiplication, the scaling factor of the result is the sum of the scaling factors of the products. This is analogous to engineering notation, where we learn to add the powers of 10.

In division, the scaling factor of the result is the difference between the scaling factor of the dividend and the scaling factor of the divisor. The scaling factor of the remainder is that of the dividend. In engineering notation, we subtract the powers of 10 for a division.

In a normal form for a signed integer, the most significant bit is one. This says, in essence, that all leading zeros have been squeezed out of the number. The sign bit does not take part in this procedure. However, note that if we know that the most significant bit is always a one, there is no reason to store it. This gives us a free bit in a sense; the most significant bit is a 1 by definition, and the msb-1-th bit is adjacent to the sign bit. This simple trick has doubled the effective accuracy of the word, because each bit position is a factor of two.

The primary operation that will cause a loss of precision or accuracy is the subtraction of two numbers that have nearly but not quite identical values. This is commonly encountered in digital filters, for example, where successive readings are differenced. For an 18 bit word, if the readings differ in, say, the 19th bit position, then the difference will be seen to be zero. On the other hand, the scaling factor of the parameters must allow sufficient range to hold the largest number expected. Care must be taken in subtracting values known to be nearly identical. Precision can be retained by pre-normalization of the arguments.

During an arithmetic operation, if the result is a value larger than the greatest positive value for a particular format, or less than the most negative, then the operation has overflowed the format. Normally, the absolute value function cannot overflow, with the exception of the absolute value of the least negative number, which has no corresponding

142

positive representation, because we made room for the representation of zero.

In addition, the scaling factor can increase by one, if we consider the possibility of adding two of the largest possible numbers. We can also consider subtracting the largest (absolute value) negative number from the largest (in an absolute sense) negative number.

A one bit position left shift is equivalent to multiplying by two. Thus, after a one position shift, the scaling factor must be adjusted to reflect the new position of the binary point. Similarly, a one bit position right shift is equivalent to division by two, and the scaling factor must be similarly adjusted after the operation.

Numeric overflow occurs when a nonzero result of an arithmetic operation is too small in absolute value to be represented. The result is usually reported as zero. The subtraction case discussed above is one example. Taking the reciprocal of the largest positive number is another.

As in the decimal representation, some numbers cannot be represented exactly in binary, regardless of the precision. Non-terminating fractions such as 1/3 are one case, and the irrational numbers such as e and pi are another. Operations involving these will result in inexact results, regardless of the format. However, this is not necessarily an error. The irrationals, by definition, cannot exactly be represented by a ratio of integers. Even in base 10 notation, e and pi extend indefinitely.

When the results of a calculation do not fix within the format, we must throw something away. We normally delete bits from the right (or low side) side of the word (the precision end). There are several ways to do this. If we simply ignore the bits that won't fit within the format, we are truncating, or rounding toward zero. We choose the closest word within the format to represent the results. We can also round up by adding 1 to the LSB of the resultant word if the first bit we're going to throw away is a 1. We can also choose to round to even, round to odd, round to nearest, round towards zero, round towards + infinity, or round towards - infinity. Consistency is the desired feature.

If we look at typical physical constants, we can get some idea of the dynamic range that we'll require for typical applications. The mass of an electron, you recall, is 9.1085×10^{-31} grams. Avogadro's number is 6.023×10^{23}. If we want to multiply these quantities, we need a dynamic range of

$10^{(23+31)} = 10^{54}$, which would require a 180 bit word (10^{54} approx.= 2^{180}). Most of the bits in this 180 bit word would be zeros as place holders. Well, since zeros don't mean anything, can't we get rid of them? Of course.

We need dynamic range, and we need precision, but we usually don't need them simultaneously. The floating point data structure will give us dynamic range, at the cost of being unable to exactly represent data.

So, finally, we talk about floating point. In essence, we need a format for the computer to work with that is analogous to engineering notation, a mantissa and a power of ten. The two parts of the word, with their associated signs, will take part in calculation exactly like the scaled integers discussed previously. The exponent is the scaling factor that we used. Whereas in scaled integers, we had a fixed scaling factor, in floating point, we allow the scaling factor to be carried along with the word, and to change as the calculations proceed.

The representation of a number in floating point, like the representation in scientific notation, is not unique. For example,

$6.54 \times 10^2 = .654 \times 10^3 = 654. \times 10^0$

We have to choose a scheme and be consistent. What is normally done is that the exponent is defined to be a number such that the leftmost digit is non-zero. This is defined as the normal form.

In the floating point representation, the number of bits assigned to the exponent determines dynamic range, and the number of bits assigned to the mantissa determine the precision, or resolution. For a fixed word size, we must allocate the available bits between the precision (mantissa), and the range (exponent).

Granularity is defined as the difference between representable numbers. This term is normally equal to the absolute precision, and relates to the least significant bit.

Denormalized numbers

This topic is getting well into the number of theory, and I will only touch on these special topics here. There is a use for numbers that are not in normal form, so-called de-normals. This has to do with decreasing granularity, and the fact that numbers in the range between zero and the smallest normal number. A denorm has an exponent which is the smallest

144

representable exponent, with a leading digit of the mantissa not equal to zero. An un-normalized number, on the other hand, has the same mantissa case, but an exponent which is not the smallest representable. Let's get back to engineering...

Overflow and Underflow

If the result of an operation results in a number too large (in an absolute magnitude case) to be represented, we have generated an overflow. If the result is too small to be represented, we have an underflow. Results of an overflow can be reported as infinity (+ or - as required), or as an error bit pattern. The underflow case is where we have generated a denormalized number. The IEEE standard, discussed below, handles denorms as valid operands. Another approach is to specify resultant denorms as zero.

Standards

There are many standards for the floating point representation, with the IEEE standard being the defacto industry choice. In this section, we'll discuss the IEEE standard in detail, and see how some other industry standards differ, and how conversions can be made.

IEEE floating point

The IEEE standard specifies the representation of a number as +/- mantissa x $2^{(+/-\ exponent)}$. Note that there are two sign bits, one for the mantissa, and one for the exponent. Note also that the exponent is an exponent of two, not ten. This is referred to as radix-2 representation. Other radices are possible. The most significant bit of the mantissa is assumed to be a 1, and is not stored. Now, let's take a look at what this representation buys us. A 16 bit integer can cover a range of +/- 10^4. A 32 bit integer can span a range of +/- 10^9. The IEEE short real format, in 32 bits, can cover a range of +/- $10^{+/-38}$. A 64 bit integer covers the range +/- 10^{19}. A long real IEEE floating point number covers the range +/- $10^{+/-\ 308}$. The dynamic range of calculations has been vastly increased for the same data size. What we have lost is the ability to exactly represent numbers, but we are close enough for engineering.

In the short, real format, the 32 bit word is broken up into fields. The mantissa, defined as a number less than 1, occupies 23 bits. The most significant bit of the data item is the sign of the mantissa. The exponent occupies 8 bits. The represented word is as follows:

$$(-1)^S (2^{E+bias}) (F1...F23)$$

where F0...F23 < 1. Note that F0=1 by definition, and is not stored.

The term $(-1)^S$ gives us + when the S bit is 0 and - when the S bit is 1. The bias term is defined as 127. This is used instead of a sign bit for the exponent, and achieves the same results. This format simplifies the hardware, because only positive numbers are then involved in exponent calculations. As a side benefit, this approach ensures that reciprocals of all representable numbers can be represented.

In the long real format, the structure is as follows:

$$(-1)^S (2^{E+bias}) (F1...F52)$$

where F0...F52 < 1. Note that F0=1 by definition, and is not stored.

Here, the bias term is defined as 1023.

For intermediate steps in a calculation, there is a temporary real data format in 80 bits. This expands the exponent to 15 bits, and the mantissa to 64 bits. This allows a range of +/- 10^{4932}, which is a large number in anyone's view.

In the IEEE format, provision is made for entities known as Not-A-Numbers (NaN's). For sample, the result of trying to multiply zero times infinity is NaN. These entities are status signals that particular violation cases took place. IEEE representation also supports four user selectable rounding modes. What do we do with results that won't fit in the bits allocated? Do we round or truncate? If we round, is it towards +/- infinity, or zero? Not all implementations of the IEEE standard implement all of the modes and options.

Floating Point References

1) "Computer Number Systems & Arithmetic", Scott, 1985, Prentice-Hall, ISBN-0-13-164211-1.

2) "Digital Computer Arithmetic Design and Implementation", Cavanagh, 1984, McGraw Hill, ISBN 0-07-010282-1.

3) "Computer Arithmetic, Principles, Architecture, and Design", Hwang, Wiley, 1979

4) Parker, "Am29027 Handbook", AMD, 1989.

5) "MC68881/882 Floating Point Coprocessor User's Manual", 1989, 2nd Ed. , Motorola, Prentice-Hall, ISBN 0-13-567009-8.

6) "80387 Programmer's Reference Manual", 1987, Intel, 231917-001.

7) "32 bit Microprogrammable Products, Am29C300/29300 Data Book, 1988, AMD.

8) Rowen, Johnson, and Ries "The MIPS R3010 Floating Point Coprocessor", IEEE Micro, June 1988.

9) DSP96002 IEEE Floating-Point Dual Port Processor User's Manual, Motorola, DSP96002um/ad, 1989.

11) ANSI/IEEE Standard 754-1985 for Binary Floating-Point Arithmetic, IEEE Computer, Jan. 1980.

12) Barrenechea, Mark J.; "Numeric Exception Handling", Programmer's Journal, MAY 01 1991 v 9 n 3 Page: 40.

13) Goldberg, David *What Every Computer Scientist Should Know About Floating-Point Arithmetic*, March, 1991 issue, Computing Surveys. Copyright 1991, Association for Computing Machinery, Inc.

14) Coonen, Jerome T. *An Implementation Guide to a Proposed Standard for Floating-Point Arithmetic*, Jan. 1980, IEEE.

MMX Extensions

The Pentium processors introduced a single-instruction multiple-data (SIMD) extension to the architecture called MMX, MultiMedia Extension, in 1997. It includes eight new 64-bit registers. These registers are meant to hold eight 8-bit integers, four 16-bit integers, or two 32-bit integers, which will be operated upon in parallel.

The MMX registers are actually mapped into the floating point registers, making it tricky to do floating point and MMX operations simultaneously. The floating point registers are 80 bits wide, and the MMX registers use the lower 64 bits. The MMX extension has continued in the IA-32, but a more SIMD operations for graphics are now included on the graphics cards.

MMX supports saturation arithmetic. In this scheme, all operations are limited to a fixed range between a defined minimum and maximum. Values beyond those limits are not recognized. The mathematical properties of associativity and distributivity are not applicable in saturation arithmetic. An alternative to saturation arithmetic is where the values wrap-around, which unfortunately changes the sign in twos-complement representation. For audio processing (louder-than-loud) and video processing (blacker-than-black), saturation arithmetic works fine. It's the issue of getting an answer "close enough) in the time allowed. Saturation arithmetic plays an important role in digital signal processing techniques for video and audio processing.

In 1997, AMD released an enhanced MMX architecture called 3DNow! which added 32-bit floating point to MMX's integer operations.

In 1999, Intel went to the SSE architecture with the Pentium-III, and later the SSE2 with the Pentium 4. This refers to Streaming SSE has new 128-bit registers, and corresponding instructions. An SSE and a floating point instruction cannot be issued in the same cycle, due to resource conflicts. SSE2 brought double precision floating point support. SSE has 70 additional instructions to support operations from digital signal processing and graphics.

Up until SSE4 was defined and implemented, with subsequent generations bring more capabilities. SSE3 added new digital signal processing features, and SSE4 added an instruction for vector dot product.

Advanced Vector Extensions (AVX) introduces a 256-bit data path, and 3-operand instructions.

Glossary of Terms and Acronyms

1's complement – a binary number representation scheme for negative values.

2's complement – another binary number representation scheme for negative values.

Accumulator – a register to hold numeric values during and after an operation.

ACM – Association for Computing Machinery; professional organization.

Ada – a programming language named after Ada Augusta, Countess of Lovelace, and daughter of Lord Byron; arguably, the first programmer. Collaborator with Charles Babbage.

ALU – arithmetic logic unit.

ANSI – American National Standards Institute

API – application program interface; specification for software modules to communicate.

ArpaNet – Advanced Research Projects Agency (U.S.), first packet switched network, 1968.

ASCII - American Standard Code for Information Interchange, a 7-bit code; developed for teleprinters.

ASIC – application specific integrated circuit, custom or semicustom,.

Assembly language – low level programming language specific to a particular ISA.

Async – asynchronous; using different clocks.

Babbage, Charles –early 19th century inventor of mechanical computing machinery to solve difference equations, and output typeset results; later machines would be fully programmable.

Baud – symbol rate; may or may not be the same as bit rate.

BCD – binary coded decimal. 4-bit entity used to represent 10 different decimal digits; with 6 spare states.

Big-endian – data format with the most significant bit or byte at the lowest address, or transmitted first.

Binary – using base 2 arithmetic for number representation.

BIOS – basic input output system; first software run after boot.

BIST – built-in self test.

Bit – smallest unit of digital information; two states.

Blackbox – functional device with inputs and outputs, but no detail on the internal workings.

Boolean – a data type with two values; an operation on these data types; named after George Boole, mid-19th century inventor of Boolean algebra.

Bootstrap – a startup or reset process that proceeds without external intervention.

Buffer – a temporary holding location for data.

Bug – an error in a program or device.

Bus – data channel, communication pathway for data transfer.

Byte – ordered collection of 8 bits; values from 0-255

C – programming language from Bell Labs, circa 1972.

Cache – faster and smaller intermediate memory between the processor and main memory.

Cache coherency – process to keep the contents of multiple caches consistent,

CAS – column address strobe (in DRAM refreshing)

Chip – integrated circuit component.

Clock – periodic timing signal to control and synchronize operations.

CMOS – complementary metal oxide semiconductor; a technology using both positive and negative semiconductors to achieve low power operation.

Complement – in binary logic, the opposite state.

Compilation – software process to translate source code to assembly or machine code (or error codes).

Control Flow – computer architecture involving directed flow through the program; data dependent paths are allowed.

Coprocessor – another processor to supplement the operations of the main processor. Used for floating point, video, etc. Usually relies on the main processor for instruction fetch; and control.

Core – early non-volatile memory technology based on ferromagnetic toroid's.

Cots – commercial, off-the-shelf.

CPU – central processing unit.

Dataflow – computer architecture where a changing value forces recalculation of dependent values.

Datagram – message on a packet switched network; the delivery, arrival time, and order of arrival are not guaranteed.

DDR – dual data rate (memory).

Deadlock – a situation in which two or more competing actions are each waiting for the other to finish, and thus neither ever does.

DCE – data communications equipment; interface to the network.

Denorm – in floating point representation, a non-zero number with a magnitude less than the smallest normal number.

Device driver – specific software to interface a peripheral to the operating system.

Digital – using discrete values for representation of states or numbers.

Dirty bit – used to signal that the contents of a cache have changed.

DMA - direct memory access (to/from memory, for I/O devices).

Double word – two words; if word = 8 bits, double word = 16 bits.

Dram – dynamic random access memory.

DTE – data terminal equipment; communicates with the DCE to get to the network.

DVI – digital visual interface (for video).

EIA – Electronics Industry Association.

Epitaxial – in semiconductors, have a crystalline overlayer with a well-defined orientation.

Eprom – erasable programmable read-only memory.

EEprom – electrically erasable read-only memory.

Ethernet – 1980's networking technology. IEEE 802.3.

Exception – interrupt due to internal events, such as overflow.

FET – field effect transistor.

Fetch/execute cycle – basic operating cycle of a computer; fetch the instruction, execute the instruction.

Firewire – serial communications protocol (IEEE-1394).

Firmware – code contained in a non-volatile memory.

Fixed point – computer numeric format with a fixed number of digits or bits, and a fixed radix point. Integers.

Flag – a binary indicator.

Flash memory – a type of non-volatile memory, similar to EEprom.

Flip-flop – a circuit with two stable states; ideal for binary.

Floating point – computer numeric format for real numbers; has significant digits and an exponent.

FPGA – field programmable gate array.

FPU – floating point unit, an ALU for floating point numbers.

Full duplex – communication in both directions simultaneously.

Gate – a circuit to implement a logic function; can have multiple inputs, but a single output.

Giga - 10^9 or 2^{30}

GPU – graphics processing unit. ALU for graphics data.

GUI – graphics user interface.

Half-duplex – communications in two directions, but not simultaneously.

Handshake – co-ordination mechanism.

Harvard architecture – memory storage scheme with separate instructions and data.

Hexadecimal – base 16 number representation.

Hexadecimal point – radix point that separates integer from fractional values of hexadecimal numbers.

IDE – Integrated development environment for software.

IEEE – Institute of Electrical and Electronic Engineers. Professional organization and standards body.

IEEE-754 – standard for floating point representation and operations.

Infinity - the largest number that can be represented in the number system.

Integer – the natural numbers, zero, and the negatives of the natural numbers.

Interrupt – an asynchronous event to signal a need for attention (example: the phone rings).

Interrupt vector – entry in a table pointing to an interrupt service routine; indexed by interrupt number.

I/O – Input-output from the computer to external devices, or a user interface.

IP – intellectual property; also internet protocol.

ISA – instruction set architecture, the software description of the computer.

ISO – International Standards Organization.

ISR – interrupt service routine, a subroutine that handles a particular interrupt event.

JTAG – Joint Test Action Group; industry group that lead to IEEE 1149.1, Standard Test Access Port and Boundary-Scan Architecture.

Junction – in semiconductors, the boundary interface of the n-type and p-type material.

Kernel – main portion of the operating system. Interface between the applications and the hardware.

Kilo – a prefix for 10^3 or 2^{10}

LAN – local area network.

Latency – time delay.

List – a data structure.

Little-endian – data format with the least significant bit or byte at the highest address, or transmitted last.

Logic operation – generally, negate, AND, OR, XOR, and their inverses.

Loop-unrolling – optimization of a loop for speed at the cost of space.

LRU – least recently used; an algorithm for item replacement in a cache.

LSB – least significant bit or byte.

LUT – look up table.

Mac – media access control; a mac address is unique on a network.

Machine language – native code for a particular computer hardware.

Mainframe – a computer you can't lift.

Mantissa – significant digits (as opposed to the exponent) of a floating point value.

Master-slave – control process with one element in charge. Master status may be exchanged among elements.

Math operation – generally, add, subtract, multiply, divide.

Mega - 10^6 or 2^{20}

Memory leak – when a program uses memory resources but does not return them, leading to a lack of available memory.

Memory scrubbing – detecting and correcting bit errors.

Mesh – a highly connected network.

MESI – modified, exclusive, shared, invalid state of a cache coherency protocol.

Metaprogramming – programs that produce or modify other programs.

Microcode – hardware level data structures to translate machine instructions into sequences of circuit level operations.

Microcontroller – microprocessor with included memory and/or I/O.

Microkernel – operating system which is not monolithic. So functions execute in user space.

Microprocessor – a monolithic cpu on a chip.

Microprogramming – modifying the microcode.

MIL-STD-1553 – military standard (US) for a serial communications bus for avionics.

MIMD – multiple instruction, multiple data

Minicomputer – smaller than a mainframe, larger than a pc.

Minix – Unix-like operating system; free and open source.

MIPS – millions of instructions per second; sometimes used as a measure of throughput.

MMU – memory management unit; translates virtual to physical addresses.

Modem – modulator/demodulator; digital communications interface for analog channels.

MRAM – Magnetorestrictive random access memory. Non-volatile memory approach using magnetic storage elements and integrated circuit fabrication techniques.

MSB – most significant bit or byte.

Multiplex – combining signals on a communication channel by sampling.

Mutex – a data structure and methodology for mutual exclusion.

Multicore – multiple processing cores on one substrate or chip; need not be identical.

NAN – not-a-number; invalid bit pattern.

NAND – negated (or inverse) AND function.

NASA – National Aeronautics and Space Administration.

NDA – non-disclosure agreement; legal agreement protecting IP.

Nibble – 4 bits, ½ byte.

NIST – National Institute of Standards and Technology (US), previously, National Bureau of Standards.

NMI – non-maskable interrupt; cannot be ignored by the software.

NOR – negated (or inverse) OR function

Normalized number – in the proper format for floating point representation.

Null modem – acting as two modems, wired back to back. Artifact of the RS-232 standard.

NUMA – non-uniform memory access for multiprocessors; local and global memory access protocol.

NVM – non-volatile memory.

Octal – base 8 number.

Off-the-shelf – commercially available; not custom.

Opcode – part of a machine language instruction that specifies the operation to be performed.

Open source – methodology for hardware or software development with free distribution and access.

Operating system – software that controls the allocation of resources in a computer.

OSI – Open systems interconnect model for networking, from ISO.

Overflow - the result of an arithmetic operation exceeds the capacity of the destination.

Packet – a small container; a block of data on a network.

Paging – memory management technique using fixed size memory blocks.

Paradigm – a pattern or model

Paradigm shift – a change from one paradigm to another. Disruptive or evolutionary.

Parallel – multiple operations or communication proceeding simultaneously.

Parity – an error detecting mechanism involving an extra check bit in the word.

PC – personal computer, politically correct, program counter.

PCB – printed circuit board.

PCI – peripheral interconnect interface (bus).

Peta - 10^{15} or 2^{50}

Pinout – mapping of signals to I/O pins of a device.

Pipeline – operations in serial, assembly-line fashion.

Pixel – picture element; smallest addressable element on a display or a sensor.

Posix – portable operating system interface, IEEE standard.

PROM – programmable read-only memory.

Quad word – four words. If word = 16 bits, quad word is 64 bits.

Queue – first in, first out data buffer structure; hardware of software.

RAID – random array of inexpensive disks; using commodity disk drives to build large storage arrays.

Radix point – separates integer and fractional parts of a real number.

RAM – random access memory; any item can be access in the same time as any other.

RAS – Row address strobe, in dram refresh.

Register – temporary storage location for a data item.

Reset – signal and process that returns the hardware to a known, defined state.

RISC – reduced instruction set computer.

ROM – read only memory.

Router – networking component for packets.

Real-time – system that responds to events in a predictable, bounded time.

RS-232 – EIA telecommunications standard (1962), serial with handshake.

SAM – sequential access memory, like a magnetic tape.

SATA – serial ATA, a storage media interconnect.

Sandbox – an isolated and controlled environment to run untested or potentially malicious code.

SDRAM – synchronous dynamic random access memory.

Segmentation – dividing a network or memory into sections.

Self-modifying code – computer code that modifies itself as it run; hard to debug

Semiconductor – material with electrical characteristics between conductors and insulators; basis of current technology processor and memory devices.

Semaphore –signaling element among processes.

Serial – bit by bit.

Server – a computer running services on a network.

Shift – move one bit position to the left or right in a word.

Sign-magnitude – number representation with a specific sign bit.

Signed number – representation with a value and a numeric sign.

SIMD – single instruction, multiple data.

Simm – single in-line memory module.

SOC – system on chip

Software – set of instructions and data to tell a computer what to do.

SMP – symmetric multiprocessing.

Snoop – monitor packets in a network, or data in a cache

SRAM – static random access memory.

Stack – first in, last out data structure. Can be hardware of software.

Stack pointer – a reference pointer to the top of the stack.

State machine – model of sequential processes.

Superscalar – computer with instruction-level parallelism, by replication of resources.

Synchronous – using the same clock to coordinate operations.

System – a collection of interacting elements and relationships with a specific behavior.

Table – data structure. Can be multi-dimensional.

Tera - 10^{12} or 2^{40}

Test-and-set – coordination mechanism for multiple processes that allows reading to a location and writing it in a non-interruptible manner.

TCP/IP – transmission control protocol/internet protocol; layered set of protocols for networks.

Thread – smallest independent set of instructions managed by a multiprocessing operating system.

TLB – translation lookaside buffer – a cache of addresses.

Transceiver – receiver and transmitter in one box.

TRAP – exception or fault handling mechanism in a computer; an operating system component.

Triplicate – using three copies (of hardware, software, messaging, power supplies, etc.). for redundancy and error control.

Truncate – discard. Cutoff, make shorter.

TTL – transistor-transistor logic in digital integrated circuits. (1963)

UART – universal asynchronous receiver-transmitter. Parallel-to-serial; serial-to parallel device with handshaking.

UDP – User datagram protocol; part of the Internet Protocol.

USART – universal synchronous (or) asynchronous receiver/transmitter.

Underflow – the result of an arithmetic operation is smaller than the smallest representable number.

USB – universal serial bus.

Unsigned number – a number without a numeric sign.

Vector – single dimensional array of values.

VHDL- very high level description language; a language to describe integrated circuits and asic/ fpga's.

VIA – vertical conducting pathway through an insulating layer in a semiconductor.

Virtual memory – memory management technique using address translation.

Virtualization – creating a virtual resource from available physical resources.

Virus – malignant computer program.

VLIW – very long instruction word – mechanism for parallelism.

von Neumann – John, a computer pioneer and mathematician; realized that computer instructions are data.

Watchdog – hardware/software function to sanity check the hardware, software, and process; applies corrective action if a fault is detected; fail-safe mechanism.

Wiki – the Hawaiian word for "quick." Refers to a collaborative content website.

Word – a collection of bits of any size; does not have to be a power of two.

Write-back – cache organization where the data is not written to main memory until the cache location is needed for re-use.

Write-only – of no interest.

Write-through – all cache writes also go to memory.

X86 – Intel -16, -32, 64-bit ISA.

XOR – exclusive OR; either but not both

Selected Bibliography

Computer Architecture, General

Bell, C. Gordon and Newell, Allen, *Computer Structures: Readings and Examples,* McGraw-Hill Inc., January 1, 1971, ISBN-0070043574.

Blaauw, Gerrit A. and Brooks, Frederick P. Jr. *Computer Architecture, Concepts and Evolution*, 2 volumes, 1997, Addison-Wesley, IBN 0-201-10557-8.

Boole, George *An Investigation of the Laws of Thought on which are Founded the Mathematical Theories of Logic and Probability,*1854. Reprinted 1958, Dover, ISBN 0-486-60028-9.

Bryant, Randal E. and O'Hallaron, David R. Computer systems: A Programmer's Perspective, 2nd edition, Addison Wesley, Kindle e-book edition, ASIN: B004S81RXE.

Burks, Arthur; W. Goldstein, Herman H.; Von Neumann, John Preliminary Discussion of the Logical Design of an Electronic Computing Instrument, 1987, MIT Press, originally published in Papers of John Von Neumann on Computing and Computer Theory.

Carter, Nick Schaum's *Outline of Computer Architecture*, McGraw-Hill; 1st edition (December 26, 2001) ISBN- 007136207X.

Comer, Douglas E. *Essentials of Computer Architecture*, Prentice Hall; US Ed edition (August 23, 2004) ISBN 0131491792.

Englander, Irv *The Architecture of Computer Hardware and Systems Software: An Information Technology Approach*, Wiley; 3 edition (January 20, 2003) ISBN-0471073253.

Everett, R. R. and Swain, F. E. *Project Whirlwind, Report R-127, Whirlwind I Computer,* Servomechanisms Laboratory, M.I.T., Sept 4, 1947.

Flores, Ivan *The Logic of Computer Arithmetic,* 1963, Prentice-Hall, ISBN 0135400392.

Harris, David and Harris, Sarah *Digital Design and Computer Architecture*, Morgan Kaufmann (March 2, 2007) ISBN 0123704979.

Hennessy, John L. and Patterson, David A. *Computer Architecture, Fifth Edition: A Quantitative Approach*, Morgan Kaufmann; (September 30, 2011) ISBN 012383872X.

Heuring, Vincent, and Jordan, Harry F. *Computer Systems Design and Architecture* (2nd Edition), Prentice Hall; 2 edition (December 6, 2003) ISBN 0130484407.

Johnson, William M. *Superscalar Microprocessors Design*, Prentice Hall PTR; Facsimile edition (December 11, 1990) ISBN 0138756341.

Kidder, Tracy *The Soul of a New Machine*, Back Bay Books (June 2000) ISBN 0316491977.

Mano, M. Morris *Computer System Architecture* (3rd Edition), Prentice Hall; 3rd edition (October 29, 1992) ISBN 0131755633.

Murdocca, Miles J. and Heuring, Vincent *Computer Architecture and Organization: An Integrated Approach*, Wiley (March 16, 2007) ISBN 0471733881.

Nisan, Noam and Schocken, Shimon, *The Elements of Computing Systems: Building a Modern Computer from First Principles*, 2005, MIT Press, ISBN 0262640686.

Null, Linda *The Essentials of Computer Organization And Architecture*, Jones & Bartlett Pub; 2 edition (February 15, 2006) ISBN 0763737690.

Page, Daniel, *A Practical Introduction to Computer Architecture*, 2009, Springer, ISBN 1848822553.

163

Patterson, David A and Hennessy, John L. *Computer Organization and Design: The Hardware/Software Interface*, Revised Fourth Edition, Morgan Kaufmann; Nov. 2011 ISBN 0123744938.

Ramachandran, Umakishore, and Leahy William D. Jr., *Computer Systems: An Integrated Approach to Architecture and Operating Systems*, 2010, Addison Wesley, ISBN 0321486137.

Reid, T. R. *The Chip: How Two Americans Invented the Microchip and Launched a Revolution*, Random House Trade Paperbacks; Revised edition (October 9, 2001) ISBN 0375758283.

Richards, R. K. *Arithmetic Operations in Digital Computers, 1955, Van Nostrand,* B00128Z00.

Schmid, Hermann *Decimal Computation*, 1974, Wiley, ISBN 0-471-76180-X.

Shriver, Bruce D. *The Anatomy of a High-Performance Microprocessor: A Systems Perspective*, Wiley-IEEE Computer Society Press (June 4, 1998) ISBN 0818684003.

Silc, Jurji, Robic, Borut, Ungerer, Theo *Processor Architecture: From Dataflow to Superscalar and Beyond*, Springer; 1 edition (July 20, 1999) ISBN 3540647988.

Stakem, Patrick H. *A Practitioner's Guide to RISC Microprocessor Architecture*, Wiley-Interscience (April 12, 1996) ISBN 0471130184.

Stallings, William *Computer Organization and Architecture: Designing for Performance* (7th Edition), Prentice Hall; 7 edition (July 21, 2005) ISBN 0131856448.

Stokes, Jon, *Inside the Machine An Illustrated Introduction to Microprocessors and Computer Architecture*, 2006, No Starch Press, ISBN 1593271042.

the conditions of the Creative commons Attribution-ShareAlike #.0 Unported License.

X86 specific

Able, Peter, IBM Assembly Language and Programming,1987, Prentice-Hall, ISBN 0-13-448143-7.

Abrash, Michael *Zen of Assembly Language*, 1990, Scott Foresman Trade, ISBN 0-673-38602-3.

Agarwal, Rakesh K. *80X86 Architecture and Programming: Architecture Reference : Covers Implementations from the 8086 to the 1486, and Includes the 80X87 Processor,* Prentice Hall (January 1991), ISBN-10: 0132454327.

Antonakos, James L. *Introduction to the Intel Family of Microprocessors: A Hands-On Approach Utilizing the 80x86 Microprocessor Family* (3rd Edition), Prentice Hall; 3rd edition (June 3, 1998), ISBN-10: 0138934398.

Brey, Barry B. *Intel 32-Bit Microprocessor: 80386, 80486, and Pentium* Prentice Hall; 1 edition (September 16, 1994), ISBN-10: 002314260X.

Brey, Barry B. *Intel Microprocessors 8086/8088, 80186, 80286, 80386, 80486, The: Architecture, Programming, and Interfacing,* Prentice Hall; 4 edition (November 18, 1996), ISBN-10: 0132606704.

Brey, Barry B. *Advanced Intel Microprocessors: 80286, 80386, And 80486,* Merrill Pub Co (August 1992), ISBN-10: 0023142456.

Brumm, Penn; Brumm, Don; Scanlon, Leo J. *80486 Programming*, Windcrest, 1991, ISBN 0-8306-7577-9.

Detmer, Richard C. *Introduction to 80X86 Assembly Language and Computer Architecture* Jones & Bartlett Pub; (February 2001), ISBN-10: 0763717738.

Duncan, Ray *MS-DOS Functions*, Microsoft Press, 1988,$5.95, ISBN 1-55615-128-4.

Duncan, Ray *IBM ROM BIOS*, Microsoft Press, 1988, $5.95, ISBN 1-55615-135-7.

165

Edelhart, Michael *Intel's Official Guide to 386 Computing,* McGraw-Hill Osborne Media (March 1991), ISBN-10: 0078816939.

Evans, James S.; Trimper, Gregory L. *Itanium Architecture for Programmers: Understanding 64-Bit Processors and EPIC Principles,* Prentice Hall; 1 edition (May 8, 2003), ISBN-10: 0131013726.

Hahn, Harley *Assembler Inside & Out,*1992, McGraw-Hill, ISBN 0-07-881842-7.

Hogan, Thom The Programmer's PC Sourcebook, Thom Hogan, 1988, Microsoft Press, ISBN 1-55615-118-7.

Holzner, Steven *Advanced Assembly Language*, Brady Books, 1991, ISBN 0-13-658774-7.

Hummel, Robert L. *Programmer's Technical Reference: the Processor and Coprocessor,* 1992, Ziff-Davis, ISBN 1-56276-016-5.

Hyde, Randall "The Art of Assembly Language Programming," 1996, http://www.arl.wustl.edu/~lockwood/class/cs306/books/artofasm/toc.html, University of California, Riverside.

Intel, *80286 and 80287 Programmer's Reference Manual*, Intel, 1987, 210498.

Intel, *80286 Hardware Reference Manual*, Intel, 210760.

Intel, *80286 Operating Systems Writer's Guide*, 121960.

Intel, 80387 Programmer's Reference Manual, 1987 ISBN 1-55512-057-1.

Intel, 80386 System Software Writer's Guide, 1987, 231499.

Intel i486 Microprocessor, 1989, 240440-001.

Intel, *80386 Programmer's Reference Manual*, Intel, 1987, ISBN 1-55512-057-1.

Irvine, Kip R. *Assembly Language for x86 Processors* Prentice Hall; 6 edition (March 7, 2010), ISBN-10: 013602212X.

Jourdain, Robert *Programmer's Problem Solver for the IBM PC, XT & AT*, Brady Books, 1986, $22.95, ISBN 0-89303-787-7.

Leinecker, Richard C. "Processor-Detection Schemes," Dr. Dobb's Journal, JUN 01 1993 v 18 i 6 p 46.

Mazidi, Muhammad Ali; Gillispie-Mazidi , Janice *80X86 IBM PC and Compatible Computers: Assembly Language, Design, and Interfacing* Volumes I & II (4th Edition), Prentice Hall; 4 edition (August 31, 2002), ISBN-10: 013061775X.

Messmer, Hans-Peter, *The Indispensable PC Hardware Book, 4th ed, 2001,* Addison Wesley, ISBN 0201596164.

Morse, Stephan and Albert, Douglas *The 80286 Architecture,* Wiley Books, 1986, ISBN 0 471-83185-9.

Myers, Ben "Some Assembly Still Required," PC Tech Journal, 03/01/89.

Norton, Peter *Inside the IBM PC,* Brady Books, 1986, ISBN 0-89303-583-1.

Norton, Peter *Programmer's Guide to the IBM PC,* Microsoft Press, 1985,ISBN 0-914845-46-2.

Norton, Peter and Socha, John *Peter Norton's Assembly Language Book for the IBM PC,* Brady Books, 1986, ISBN 013-661901-0.

Rash, Bill "iAPX 286 Loadall Instruction," Intel Technical Memo, November 21, 1984.

Robinson, Phillip (ed), *Dr. Dobb's Toolbox of 80286/80386 Programming,* M&T Books, 1988, ISBN 0-934375-42-9.

Sanchez, Julio and Canton, Maria P. *IBM Microcomputers: A Programmer's Handbook,*1990, McGraw-Hill, ISBN 0070545944.

Sanchez, Julio and Canton, Maria P. *IBM Microcomputer Assembly Language in 10 Programming Lessons,* Prentice Hall, August 1991, ISBN-10: 0137264070.

Scanlon, Leo, *8086/8088 Assembly Language Programming,* Brady Books, 1984, ISBN 0-89303-424-X.

Scanlon, Leo J. *8086/8088/80286 Assembly Language,* (Revised Edition), Brady Books,1988, ISBN 0-13-246919-7.

Scanlon, Leo J. *Assembly Language Programming for the IBM pc/at,* Brady Books, 1989, ISBN 0-89303-484-3.

Shanley, Tom *Protected Mode Software Architecture,* Addison-Wesley Professional; 1 edition (March 16, 1996), ISBN-10: 020155447X.

Shanley, Tom *80486 System Architecture* (3rd Edition), Addison Wesley Longman; 3rd Sub edition, January 1995, ISBN-10: 0201409941.

Skinner, Thomas *An Introduction to Assembly Language Programming for the 8086 Family*, Wiley, 1985, $18.95,ISBN0-471-80825-3.

Strauss, Edmund *80386 Technical Reference*, Brady Books, 1987, ISBN 0-13-246893-X.

Stitt, Martin *Debugging, Creative Techniques and Tools for Software Repair,* Wiley, 1992, ISBN 0-471-55829-X.

Swan, T. *Mastering Turbo Assembler*, Hayden Books,1989, ISBN 0-672-48435-8.

Theis, Klaus-Dieter *The Innovative 80X86 Architectures: The 80286 Microprocessor,* Prentice Hall (January 1991), ISBN-10: 0134672836.

Triebel, Walter A. *The 80386, 80486, and Pentium Microprocessor: Hardware, Software, and Interfacing,* Prentice Hall; 1 edition (October 3, 1997), ISBN-10: 0135332257.

Uffenbeck, John T*he 80x86 Family: Design, Programming, and Interfacing* (3rd Edition) Prentice Hall; 3 edition (February 14, 2001), ISBN-10: 0130257117.

Van Gilluwe, Frank, *The Undocumented PC,* 1996, 2nd ed, Addison Wesley Professional, ISBN 0201479508.

Willen, David and Krantz, Jeffrey *8088 Assembler Language Programming: The IBM PC* (2nd ed), Sams, 1983, ISBN0-672-22400-3.

Wilt, Nicholas "Assembly Language Programming for the 80x87," Dr. Dobb's Journal 1992 v 17 i 3 P. 36.

Wyatt, Allen *Assembly Language Quick Reference*, Que,1989, ISBN 0-88022-428-2.

Yu, Ytha and Marut, Charles, *Assembly Language Programming and Organization of the IBM PC*, Mitchell Publishing (McGraw Hill), 1992, ISBN 0070726922.

MicroDesign Resources *,The Complete x86: The Definitive Guide to 386, 486, and the Pentium-class Microprocessors*, (1994), ISBN-10: 1885330022.

Understanding X86 Microprocessors: 99 Articles Originally Published in Microprocessor Report Between September 1987 and April 1993 Ziff Davis Press, June 1993), ISBN-10: 1562761587

Pentium

Colwell, Robert P. *The Pentium Chronicles: The People, Passion, and Politics Behind Intel's Landmark Chips,* Wiley-IEEE Computer Society Press; 1st edition, December 23, 2005, ISBN-10: 0471736171.

Feibus, Michael; "Pentium Power," PC, Apr 1993 v 12 n 8 P 108.

Halfhill, Tom R. "Intel Launches Rocket in a Socket: Intel's new Pentium CPU doubles the speed of the fastest 486," Byte, May 1993 v 18 n 6 P 92.

Miller, Micheal J. "Is There a Pentium in Your Future?" PC, Apr 1993 v 12 n 8 P81.

Smith, Gina "Field Guide to CPUs," PC/Computing, Mar 1993 v 6 n 3 P123.

Smith, Gina "Will the Pentium kill the 486?," PC/Computing, May 1993 v 6 n 5 P 116.

Subramaniam, Ramesh; Kundargi, Kira; "Programming the Pentium Processor," Dr. Dobb's Journal, Jun 1993 v 18 i 6 p 34.

Tredennick, Nick "Computer Science and the Microprocessor," Dr. Dobb's Journal, Jun 1993 v 18 i 6 p 18.

"Inside: Pentium or the 586?," PC, Apr 1993 v 12 n 8 Page: 4.

"PCI, Pentium link forged," Computer Design, Apr 1993 v 32 n 4 Page: 40.

"The Making of a Chip," Business Week, Mar 1993 n 3311 Page :94.

"The Pentium Challenge," Informationweek, Mar 1993 n 417 Page: 14.

"New Era for Intel: The Supercharged Pentium PC," Electronics, Mar 1993 v 66 n 6 P 4.

"Preparing the way for Pentium," Datamation, Mar 1993 v 39 n 6 Page: 36.

"Intel's Pentium Processor, Coming in March: one very hot CPU," PC World, Feb 1993 v 11 n 2 Page: 67.

Pentium Benchmarks, PC Week, Feb. 1993.

Pentium Processor User's Manual, 3 volume set, Intel, 1993, order 241563-001.

Ruley, John "Pentium Arrives,", Windows, Jun 1993, p. 115.

80x86 chips chart

model	company	introduction	data bus	Max word size	address bus
8086	Intel	1978	16	16	16
8087	Intel	1978	16	80	16
8088	various	1979	8	16	16
8800/i432	Intel	1981	32	32	32
80186	various	1981	16	16	16
80188	various	1981	8	16	16
80286	various	1982	16	16	24
80287	various	1982	16	80	n/a
V-20	NEC	1984	8	16	16
V-30	NEC	1984	16	16	16
80386	Intel	1985	32	32	32
80387	various	1985	32	80	n/a
AM386	AMD	1985	32	32	32
80386sx	Intel	1985	16	32	16
3c87	IIT	1989	16	80	n/a
80486	Intel	1989	32	32,80	32
AM486	AMD	1989	32	32,80	32
AM586	AMD	1989	32	32,80	32
Pentium	Intel	1993	32	32,80	32
5x86	Cyrix	1993	32	32,80	32
Nx586	Nexgen	1994	32	32	32
PentiumPro	Intel	1995	32	32,80	36
6x86	Cyrix	1995	32	32,80	36
M-II	Cyrix	1995	32	32,80	36
K5	AMD	1996	32	32,80	32
C6	IDT	1997	32	32,80	32
C3,C7	Via	1997	32	32,80	32
Pentium II	Intel	1997	32	64,80	36
K6	AMD	1997	32	32,80	36
Pentium III	Intel	1999	32	64,80	36
K7- Athlon	AMD	1999	32	32,80	36
K7 - Duron	AMD	2000	32	32,80	32
Pentium 4	Intel	2000	32	32,80	36
Crusoe	Transmeta	2000	32	32,80	36
Itanium	Intel/HP	2001	64	64,80	50
K8 - Opteron	AMD	2003	64	64,80	40
K7 - Sem-	AMD	2004	32	32,80	32

pron					
P4 Prescott	Intel	2004	64	64,80	64
Pentium-D	Intel	2005	32	32,80	
Core 2	Intel	2006	64	64,80	64
Pentium M	Intel	2006	32	32,80	36
Core	Intel	2006	32	32,80	36
Nano	Via	2008	64	64,80	64
Pentium-D	Intel	2008	32/64	64,80	

If you enjoyed this book, you might find something else from the author interesting as well. Available on Amazon Kindle, or as printed (P) copy.

Computer Architecture

4- and 8-bit Microprocessors, Architecture and History.
16-bit Microprocessors, History and Architecture.
RISC Microprocessors, History and Overview.
Floating Point Computation.
Computer Architecture and Programming of the Intel X86 Family.

The Hardware and Software Architecture of the Transputer .

The Architecture and Applications of the ARM Microprocessors.

Embedded Computer Systems, Vol. 1, Introduction and Architecture.
Embedded Computer Systems, Vol. 2, Implementing Embedded (Fall, 2015)
Architecture of Massively Parallel Microprocessor Systems.

Computer Virtualization and the Cloud.
Multicore Computer Architectures
Mainframes (Summer 2015)
Microprocessors in Space.
What's the Worst That Could Happen?: Bad Assumptions, Ignorance, Failures, and Screw-ups in Engineering Projects.

Space

The History of Spacecraft Computers from the V-2 to the Space Station
The Saturn Rocket and the Pegasus Missions.
Robots and Telerobots in Space Applications.
Microprocessors in Space
Apollo's Computers.
On Orbit Repair and Servicing of Spacecraft (Summer 2015)

www.ingramcontent.com/pod-product-compliance
Lightning Source LLC
LaVergne TN
LVHW092333060326
832902LV00008B/619